Newbie F

Make High Profits *right away* as a Forex Beginner

By Joseph Lira

Copyright 2015

Who I wrote this book for and why I wrote it

Brand new (newbie) traders all make the same mistakes over and over because *they don't know any better*, now you *do*. Newbie traders tend to do what everyone else is doing and study what everyone else is studying thus they have the same results and failures as everyone else. Don't be *that* trader! If you can just take the time to read this information in this first book in the newbie trader series, let it sink in and then continue on your educational journey you will have done yourself a *huge* favor and also begun to give yourself the needed *edge* to succeed in this business and be able to start trading **on as little as $500 capital to start with**.

I wrote **Newbie Forex Traders Bible** for all beginning aspiring investors and traders who are just getting their head around doing the day trading and swing trading business. Everyone has their own ideas of what they think day trading and swing trading are and what it can do for them. This book is for beginners and will detail many of the things that a brand new trader *must* learn *not to do* before they can become consistently profitable in the live markets. You're heard the saying "just say no to drugs", just say no to day trading and you and your account will be *waaaaay* ahead of the game to start off. Don't say I didn't warn you, OK, continue with your insanity and read this entire book to give yourself a fighting chance.

Picture yourself throwing *all* your startup capital into the bon fire at the party you'll throw for yourself for starting your new trading business up and watch it burn up in smoke and flames right before your very eyes. You smell that? That's all your money burning up because you *went to fast* or *did not learn what to do the right way* from the first day of your business and did not develop the needed edge to compete at the highest level. Trust me when I say, the sharks in the market will chomp up your trading account without hesitation. We'll get to the sharks a little later on in the book so you know *who* they are and *what* they can do to you as a brand new beginner trader.

While I love mentoring brand new traders, I have them working on daily charts learning supply and demand trading **ON DAILY CHARTS**! If you want to get into the financial market investing and trading business and you want to make money, **LOTS OF IT**, you would want to be doing what the smart money does *right*? Smart money doesn't day trade, they don't use five minute charts, and they don't try to scalp, why, because they are in this business to make money, *scads of it*!

Newbie Forex Traders Bible is going to give you the brutal truth about day trading. What was it Jack Nicholson's character Colonial Nathan Jessup said in the movie A Few Good Men? *"You can't handle the truth"*! Do you want to invest and trade with *real* information or do you want to be lied too? The only thing in investing and trading that can't lie to you is price action on your trading chart. Smart money *cannot hide* what they are doing in the market and it shows up on the price chart you look at *every day* you just need to be able to spot *what* they are doing *where* they are doing it.

This business isn't really an H&P type of business, what is H&P you might be asking, hoping and praying. You don't need a rosary you need an edge. I'm *not* going to sugar coat it, this business is an *ugly place* for an untrained and underfunded beginner. There are *very bad* people in the live market who are looking to *take all of your money* from you, and they will should you not be prepared properly to go to work in the live markets. Again, don't say I haven't tried to warn you.

You absolutely need to have a competitive edge in the markets, and you must have it *before* you do anything in the live markets with real money. I will have some other books out soon that detail how to develop your edge for making money in today's live markets, I encourage you to read them all as soon as they come out if you are in this business to make money. If you run with the 'sheeple of the herd' you can be assured to *not* have any edge. They all study the same information and are all programmed the same way to lose money repeatedly.

My hope from **Newbie Forex Traders Bible** is that you understand how *important* it is to have a competitive edge when putting your hard earned money at risk in the markets. Each day, the wealth from trader accounts is transferred from those without an edge into the accounts of those who have developed that all needed important winning edge. *Which one do you want to be?*

There are only two groups of people who are doing business in the markets, the professionals and the retail investors and traders. The retail group includes both "wanna be" traders and also brand new traders with *zero* experience at all who are just trying to be cool and say they work in the market.

Use **Newbie Forex Traders Bible** as an overview or a guide if you will, for what to study and learn first to become consistently profitable from day trading. I give you concise information as to what to learn first and what to look for as far as further information is concerned. I tell you *only* the most critical things to learn first because those are absolutely the most important and the ones that will make you money *right away* if you do them. **Newbie Forex Traders Bible** is written to provide straightforward, easy to understand and easy to apply advice, tips and techniques that can be the backbone of any successful traders success in the financial markets.

Instead of trying to read **Newbie Forex Traders Bible** fast I recommend that you *go slow* and look up and search for the main things the book talks about that will help you to *become successful right away*. Skip over anything that is important and it could for sure cause you to lose some money. No one wants that now, *right?*

I did not put all the history of financial markets and all the stats in this book. You can look all of that up online at your leisure if you want to know that information. While it is good to know, it *will not* make you real money in the live financial markets every day.

Newbie Forex Traders Bible will be an incredible read for someone who has *zero* knowledge or someone who has some basic experience who is struggling with their trading and investing. I *purposely* do not put any charts or graphs in this book and I will tell you why. This is a very good book for the novice as it is easy to absorb information. Since you're new all you need to do at this point is try to absorb what is said here.

Newbie Forex Traders Bible is about giving you the best information you need to *really* give you a fighting chance at becoming successful in this business. I try to keep industry jargon to a minimum and give links to locations where more education and training information can be found online and for ***free***. You will have plenty of time to be wowed by pretty colored charts and graphs trust me on that!

Simple, basic and easy to understand, if I can give you one word of advice at this point in this book I will tell you to keep it simple because trading *really is* simple if you keep it that way. You *do not* need any indicators or fancy systems, methods or software that the so called gurus are all touting. The market *only* works on supply and demand and supply and demand is the *only thing* that as I said earlier moves price on a chart from one value area to another. Doesn't it make sense then to study what makes the market do what it does and use that as your trading method?

To me it is a *no brainer* however most brand new investors and traders are of the notion that they need some sort of fancy system or method. As I said, keep it simple and it will be. There is no *easier* and *faster* method to learn than supply and demand so I encourage you to get right to it and learn *how* and *why* the market does what it does and then go in there and get paid from it. This book cuts right to the core and lays out a progressive foundation of principles on which you can indeed begin swing trading for high profit *as long as* you have done the education and training the right way from the first day.

Here is the first *tip* I can give you. Don't waste time on learning things that *will not* help you make money in the live market. You don't need to know the history of the financial markets and what all the old time guys who made a lot of money did to make their loot. It's not even the same market or economics as it was when they were in the live market so don't waste any valuable education and learning time on learning that information.

I encourage you to begin to learn *only* what will make you money in *today's* markets. If you would like to go back and study all that history once you have become consistently profitable on a daily basis so be it. If and when you do become successful in this business you will have a lot of time on your hands anyway because at that juncture trading is boring and it is a lot of waiting around.

In the meantime though, let's get you learning how to drive your new money train down the tracks of gold to the front door of your bank so you can deposit all the profits you are going to learn how to take out of *today's* markets. You don't need to know what happened in the market 100 years ago you need to know what is happening in the market *right now* and how to make money from it.

Learning to be a great investor and trader does not have to be a long, hard road—trust me on this. I had to unlearn a lot of things that are of no use to anyone in the live markets. I don't want you make those same errors. Let's try to *cut down* your learning curve so that you can start making real money right from the start of your new investing and trading business.

When you are done reading **Newbie Forex Traders Bible** you will have an excellent basic explanation of *what* and *what not* to do before you even study anything or do any kind of education. The information in this book will put you on the *fast track* to becoming a successful self-directed investor and trader with very little money invested other than the cost of this book.

I have tried to give you in **Newbie Forex Traders Bible** the truth of what happens in real life, in real time and in real money in the live markets every day. There are *no short cuts* and you must do the time if you want to drive your own money train. I try to keep the explanations clear concise, simple and uncomplicated. This book gives you substantial value and is going to be the foundation of your pre education for trading.

I wrote **Newbie Forex Traders Bible** for the benefit of those who want to explore investing and trading but have *no experience*, because I was incensed at how trading is taught in most books and courses so wrong and unrealistically. I have even heard industry people say that it is done intentionally so that the smart money can continue to profit. All they give you is unrealistic information that *will not* help you in the live markets using real money. *Why* would you want to learn something the wrong way from the start that could cause you to lose your hard-earned money? *To me that's just crazy.*

As a professional investor and trader, I felt it was time to show that most learning by new people in the business can be *very easy* if they learn what to do the right way from the very start of their education process.

What this book is going to tell you is how not to make the mistakes that most new investors and traders make that cause them to lose money right away.

The market is not a big secret and all of the information you need to make a trading decision is right out in the open. If you know where to find the information and know what to look for you *can* and *will* make *some* money <u>every</u> <u>day</u> in the market provided you are looking at the *right* information.

Unfortunately the trading-education industry does not have a good track record when it comes to its information practices and due to very little regulation in the industry, most people learn to trade completely wrong from someone who is good at marketing and sales but not so good at trading or who *doesn't even trade at all*. Later on I will discuss the importance of getting a mentor and how doing so can also *greatly expedite* your learning curve and help you to make real money faster.

As I have said before, there a lot of unscrupulous junkware selling locusts out there, waiting to prey on unsuspecting new investors and traders coming into the business. I am certainly *not* one them, I am not trying to sell you any fancy indicators, methods, systems or "secrets" of the financial markets. I'm not trying to shove any red or green hopium pills down your throat. I am just an honest real money trader who is giving you the best advice and information you can have right upfront *before* you make any mistakes. What you do with that information is up to you, either you *"get it"* in this business or you don't!

If anything, **Newbie Forex Traders Bible** is giving you the harsh reality as to what it will take for you to actually be able to make real money in the live market and be consistently profitable doing it. Honestly, all of us in the markets who are already doing it for real and using real money are waiting for all the new people to coming into the market so we can continue to profit.

I encourage you to read this entire book through thoroughly one time from the beginning and not skip anything. It is very important to grasp the foundational principles described as the book progresses. By skipping around you could perhaps miss a critical step or some information that is part of the order in which investing and trading needs to be learned.

Newbie Forex Traders Bible can help you keep it simple and filter the huge amount of information out there down to *only* what you need to know right away and then can work towards adding more information and studies as you go. My philosophy is to *start small and build on success* have limited exposure while you hone your skills, then progress as you become more competent.

You can use **Newbie Forex Traders Bible** and the references, suggestions and tips in it to go further into your educational studies of the markets and there dynamics. Knowing market dynamics is going to be critical for you to have the winning edge you will need to be a successful market participant. By studying what this book suggests you will not become one of the 97% of the sheeple of the herd.

This business is *no joke*. I always say there are people in the live market who will walk over dead bodies to get paid and make money so make no mistake they are in there to take *all* of *your* money. They see you, they know what mistakes you are going to make over and over and over again. This is how they get paid from the sheeple of the herd.

So *who are* these sheeple of the herd I keep talking about, **YOU**, that's who!

Sheeple of the herd! Sounds like a B horror movie or a cult doesn't it? The sheeple of the herd as I call them are the retail investors and traders from around the world who all study the same thing, do the same thing, and trade the same way as everyone else. They all trade from the same charts and make the same mistakes over and over again. They are *very easy* to see on the charts thus they are very easy targets to make money from.

I have probably scared you a little bit by now as a newbie beginner however a little fright can't hurt you at this point, what *can* though is not paying attention to what **Newbie Forex Traders Bible** is telling you *not* to do. Every time you are thinking to yourself "oh I will just come back to that" or "I will skip that because it is not important" just think about the bon fire at your party. If you want to get your new money train cruising down the tracks of gold to the front door of your bank every day, *don't skip one word of this book.*

Table of Contents

Extra links

Glossary

Disclaimer

Important factors for Forex day trading newbies – know *why* you're doing it

Begin with the end in mind I always say. There are a lot of things to consider when thinking about becoming a professional market investor and trader. You are the one who is making the decision to get into the futures trading and investing business, no one is making you do it. It is a big step for someone to take the plunge into the world of making money with money. One has to look inside one's self and ask some very hard questions before they start driving their own money train down the tracks to riches in the live markets.

It is very important to have figured out what your ultimate goals are *before* you step foot into the markets with your hard earned real money. Questions I ask new people are: are you trading for short term income or long term wealth building? Are you trying to build up your account balance to be able to take on more risk and trade larger size? I ask them *why* they want to do this business. I ask them if they know what their goals for the long term are and if they are thinking with a long term perspective.

If a new investor or trader cannot answer these questions right away I just encourage them to *stay out* of the live markets until they can answer them and be honest. I also will ask them how much capital they plan to enter the live markets to work with. There is no point in trying to enter the live markets with scared money.

Here are some of the main things you need to ask yourself and have made a decision on *before* you get going. Are you trading for short term income? Are you trading to build up an account balance so you can start trading multiple shares, lots or contracts? Are you trading for long term wealth goals and/or retirement and wish to be a *buy* and *hold* type of investor?

What kind of investor or trader do you desire to be? You should know this *before* beginning this business. Figure out what style of investing or trading suits your personality the best. Do you want to day trade, swing trade, or position trade? What kind of time are you looking to put in on a daily basis? What kind of returns are you looking at monetarily? Are you the type of person who has a lot of time to devote to looking at charts in the live market to be a day trader? While I *do not* recommend day trading, it is possible; however, it requires a lot of time, preparation and a large amount capital. I know very few successful day traders.

While I *do not* recommend day trading, it is possible; however, it requires a lot of time, preparation and a *large* amount capital. I know very few successful day traders. But if you are going to try it, **Newbie Forex Traders Bible** will tell you how you can do it with *as little as $500 to start off*.

There are only a few different ways to be a market speculator - which way is best for you? You would either become an intraday trader, a swing trader or position trader. Do you like action? Maybe you want to be a scalper and get in and out of trades very quickly and take many trades in one day. You need a speedy internet connection for this type of trading.

I am sorry to inform you that there is **no such thing** as scalping unless you are an algorithm. *Are* you an algorithm? I think not! Even *if* you could scalp you would need to be using an account size of five hundred thousand dollars or more to make it worth the costs that you would incur doing that type of trading. Don't be a kook and try it because as a retail trader you will lose **all** of your freakin money. ***ALLLLL OOOOOF ITTTTTT***!

If you want to swing trade, you will need to have the capital in your account to handle the overnight margin requirement of whatever your chosen instrument is to work in. CAUTION: If you are new and have to use leverage to trade, you just shouldn't trade. *Stay out* until you have sufficient capital to go into the market and be able to have a chance to make money.

You can also become a position investor and trader and keep positions for a long term time horizon. Most position investors and traders are in a position for months and sometimes years. These are the most successful consistently profitable money making investors and traders in the business. It is this type of investing and trading which over the long term makes the most amount of money.

One of the reasons this type of investing and trading is so profitable is because the expenses associated with this type of market action are low and do not add up as quickly as they do with other types of trading. Remember it takes money to make money and also *costs* money to make money in the live markets.

If you would like to be more of an investor or position trader, then you will also need to be well-funded to sustain a draw-down on a position of as much as 50 percent. Should you not have the mental wherewithal to sit through a 50 percent draw-down on any given position in your portfolio, then again I recommend just staying out of the live markets until you have the psychological makeup to do so.

The next thing you need to make a decision on before doing anything is how much money you plan to capitalize your new investing and trading business with. As has been said before and will be said again right here and now. *Only trade with money you can afford to lose.*

Here is a visualization you can do to get that last sentence in perspective as a newbie. Picture yourself throwing your starting capital into your barbeque, turning the barbeque all the way up to the highest flame or like we were discussing earlier throwing all your hard earned money into the bon fire at the party you're throwing for yourself for starting your new trading business then watching your money burn up in flames and smoke right before your very eyes.

I recommend picking *one style* of investing or trading and becoming an expert at it. Find a few instruments you like and study their price action and work in those exclusively. You *do not* need to work in *every* asset class there is. You also do not need to *be in* the market all the time because cash is also a position.

I *strongly* recommend you know what type of market investor or trader you desire to be and whether you will be active or passive and *before* you start to study or learn any information related to market investing. Being *well prepared* can help cut down on the long learning curve there is to becoming successful in this business.

There are a lot of serious realistic questions you must ask yourself and have answered *truthfully* before you begin in this business and especially before you put any of your hard earned money on the line in the live markets. My best advice to you in this section is to *get real* about what you think trading is. Do some research if you have not already; learn what is realistic, and what *is not* in this business. You will save yourself a lot of time *and* money. Start your trading business with realistic goals and reasonable expectations; you'll set yourself up for better success.

The more of these questions you have answered *before* you begin to do anything in this business the better prepared you will be to become successful. There are no guarantees in the market. It is all about preparedness and you are the only one making you do this business so I encourage you to listen to the advice given in this section *very carefully*. It is *strongly recommended* that you have all of the above issues resolved *before* taking *any* action with real money in the live markets.

It all starts with *you*. It also _ends_ there if you're not diligent in what you do. Once have you have decided on *how* you approach the market it is important to *stick with your decision*. Are you going to trade futures, spot Forex or Forex futures or *both*? Do you know the difference?

If you are going to trade Forex are you going to do it in the spot Forex or the Forex futures? There is a big difference at what you can *get away with* in each one and you should know the differences between them and base your decision of which to work in on the information you get from your research.

What kinds of charts do you trade futures or Forex futures on, daily, monthly, intraday? Are you a day trader, swing trader or market investor of futures or Forex futures? You should have *all* of these questions answered *before* studying anything or ever stepping foot in the live market with real money.

It is important to know *all* this information first in order to plan out what type of education and training one will do when entering the learning phase of the knowledge curve. There is a lot to know to be successful in the investing and trading business so it is crucial to know what type of market participant you would like to be in order to not waste any learning time (or hard earned money) for that matter.

What is the best job you never thought of? I bet it wasn't day trader, investor, or high frequency day trader? Was it money manager/day trader, risk manager/day trader? For the type of job I am writing about in this book there isn't even a high school diploma or MBA needed!!! Hell no clothes needed for that matter!

You absolutely *do not* need a big fancy degree from a big fancy Ivy League college to become successful at the business of making money with money. All the information you need to do this business is readily available online if you know *where* to get it. You *will* need to develop your own time management skills though. There are some extra links at the end of the book to help you expedite some of your learning curve time. You're welcome!

I will talk about where to go to get the information you need to become consistently profitable in this business a little later however right now I want to tell about how good it is to be able to do this business working for yourself.

The amount of time you want to work is up to you. You are the boss right? You make the decisions as to *when* you want to work and *for how long*. Since I position trade now I might spend 30 minutes a week analyzing my charts. I suggest if you are brand new to the trading business that you spend at least 10 minutes a day reviewing your positions at the very minimum. Could you get your head around only working 30 minutes a week and making an *unlimited* income?

You can pick the best time of day which suits your lifestyle to work in the financial markets. You can work in any session there is in which the markets are open. There are many to choose from so you have the chance to make money when it is convenient for *you*. That's the beauty of it!

Investing and trading futures is the best business in the world as far as I am concerned. It is the only business I know of where you can be at the beach on a beautiful sunny day or scuba diving or flying to Europe for the weekend to meet up with friends and still be making money the whole time you're doing it.

You want to learn to invest in and trade futures right? You want to make money and have a lot of freedom right? Do what it says in this book and you can be on your way to giving yourself and your family the best life you could ever imagine all from the comfort of your own home perhaps. I walk from my bedroom to my office and that is my commute to work for the day. *Can you get your head around that?*

I am giving you clear, concise and highly informative information in this book that would take you *years* to uncover on your own. No amount of search engine queries' could come up with all of the information I am giving you in this book in one place let alone at one time. I do not ever presume to tell you how to run your life however if you do what it says in this book your life and that of your family can be *MUCH* easier if you do it the right way the first time!

If you need to learn this business from the ground up then **Newbie Forex Traders Bible** is definitely for you. I encourage you to read it as many times as it takes for it to become clear to you as to what you do and do not need to learn to be successful in this business from the start. There are no guarantees in the markets however you must know the right information from the start to have a chance of becoming successful.

All the expenses on the wrong education you are going to save by reading this book and putting the principles to work for yourself to make money I think you could buy me a few thousand pounds of fuel for my G650. What do you say? That's a joke you can't afford G650 fuel right now but someday you will! You can do well in the markets and just get a G650 of your own.

In this book I give you brutally honest realism of investing and trading and what you need to know, the GOOD and the BAD before you even start to study anything. I tell you everything NOT to do that causes people who come into this business with dollar signs in the eyes to get FUBAR by the smart money. I give simple explanations that even a 12 year old can understand. If you read a passage in this book and it says hey "don't do this" then guess what? **DON'T DO IT**!!

When I give a reference I will put the web link to it and also tell you how to find more information and even how to word the search string for your search engine of choice. Doesn't matter which one you use as they all lead to the same data. I give you specific actions you can take to know what to do BEFORE you ever start investing or trading with real money. There are some great clickable links in the extra links section at the end of the book to give more information.

I have tried to keep this book light, fun and somewhat humorous so as not be to bossy. Learning this business does not have to be dry, tedious and boring. I wrote it as I said for the new investor and trader who has zero experience and needs a lift off point of reference. This book is it.

Terminology and industry jargon has been kept to a minimum so that if English is not your native language you are still able to fully understand and comprehend what is being spoken about. I also tried to write it in plain, simple and clear enough language so that it can be translated into any language in the world if need be.

Investing and trading in the Forex futures and futures and equities markets is a hard business to be in if you don't know what you are doing. You can lose *all* of your hard earned money in the markets if you do not take the time to do what it takes to get the right education and training the right way from the start. The learning curve in this business *AND IT IS A BUSINESS* can be long, brutal and *very very* expensive if learned the wrong way. This **Newbie Forex Traders Bible** aims to show you the right way the first time and *greatly reduce* that long learning curve by showing you what the market is really made of and *who* is actually in control of it and *when* they are in control of it.

All of the information or pieces to the puzzle if that is what you would like to call it are out there. Gordon Gekko also said "The most valuable commodity I know of is information". I also say the even beyond that is to know *how* and *where* to get that information is priceless. The professionals have learned how to do this and are experts at it in the assets they invest and trade in. They have studied and mastered the skill of knowing how to quantify price action on a chart and are able to see where the smart money has their unfilled orders residing in the live market.

The key is to know what kind of trader you desire to be and know this information first in order to plan out what type of education and training one will do when entering the learning phase of the knowledge curve. There is a lot to know to be successful in the futures investing and trading business so it is crucial to know *what type* of market participant you would like to be in order to not waste any learning time (or hard earned money) for that matter.

These next sections coming up are going to give you a *basic* understanding of reading a price chart, price action and few other skills you need to master right away. You will learn much more in-depth chart reading skills to help you make buying and selling decisions in the live markets using your real money as you progress after reading this book and completing your education and training.

The information in **Newbie Forex Traders Bible** is some of the most important information you will *ever* read in your life about trading and investing so I encourage you to read it slow and take notes if you can or if you bought the paperback of this book you can just high lite the sections you want to go back and read again.

Habits of undisciplined Forex traders – here's what *not* to do

People as I said get into this business thinking with unrealistic expectations that they are going to make millions of dollars from the start. We all thought it at least once. It is the investors and traders who develop the mindset of becoming well-off and having a great amount of freedom who are the ones who start ahead of the herd and who usually do well in the live markets.

I am not saying that you could not make millions of dollars in the markets because *you surely can*. You would just need to be using hundreds of millions of dollars to do so.

It is mostly Wall Street banks and hedge funds who are using *a lot* of leverage which is borrowed money, and OPM (other people's money) to make the profits they book. The leverage is most of the time money they borrowed from the Wall Street bankers or is it bankster's, Hmmmmm, more like loan sharks if you ask me. They also use the money you put into your IRA or your 401K and then take all of your beginning trading capital from you because you were not prepared to work with them in the live market, whose fault is that?

All the content in **Newbie Forex Traders Bible** is unique in that the information being shared here is all in one place at one time for beginners so they do not have to search around and waste a lot of time doing so. Most of us who do this business professionally are counting on the inexperienced to make all of the mistakes that this book details. It is how we make our money. We buy and sell from the retail investor and trader who have not taken the proper steps to become prepared to be successful in this business.

The most important thing about market education is learning it the right way from the beginning and *not* making the mistakes that other people are making. Don't become one of the sheeple of the herd. If you learn what *not* to do right from the very start, *you will already have an edge* over the others who did not take the time to educate themselves properly—this is whom you can actually make money from in the financial markets once you can see their fear and greed.

The decision you are making to get into the trading business is one of the most important decisions of your life. Getting into this business and becoming good enough at it to make a comfortable living from it will test your being to the very core. This is one business that will expose every flaw you have *and then some*. There is no hiding in this business, and there are people in the business *already* who know you better than you know yourself at this juncture and they are going to take complete advantage of your every flaw until you "*get it*" and become a consistently profitable professional whose using a rule based plan every day.

This section of the book details some of the reasons why 97% of all brand new day traders swing traders and also investors fail and lose all of their money. I encourage you to use this section as a reference guide as to *what not to do* to prepare to work in the live market. The mistakes I detail in this book are universally made by virtually *all* brand new investors and traders because they don't have the right information from the start of their time in the business. Now you do, *you're welcome*!

So here are some of the top reasons why brand new traders fail and lose all of their money. 1. Brand new traders have unrealistic goals to start. 2. Brand new traders do not treat trading as a business. 3. Brand new traders not do proper education and training. 4. Brand new traders fail learn to read a price chart properly. 5. Brand new traders do not learn enough money management. 6. Brand new traders fail to develop their psychology for trading. 7. Brand new traders do not compose a winning rule based plan. 8. Brand new traders fail to compose a trading journal. 9. Brand traders invest and trade real money before they are ready to do so. 10. Brand new traders try to trade to many different assets. 11. Brand new traders jump from method to method. 12. Brand new traders fail to get mentoring.

If you pay strict attention to what has been detailed in this section of the book and learn what _not_ to do, you have an excellent chance of becoming a successful and profitable self-directed market participant. Should you decide *not* to listen to what it says in this book you will have a *verrrry looong* and expensive journey I assure you of that! Don't be *that* trader!

There is a certain progression of things that brand new investors and traders need to know and study. Unfortunately no one tells them in the beginning that most of the information they need is basic and is mostly common sense, *buy low sell high*. They don't usually find out until *it is too late* for their account and they have blown out or ran it down so far they cannot trade live anymore until they deposit more risk capital.

Should you decide to try to take any short cuts or side step any of the learning process, you can be assured of losing *some* or *all* of your money in the live market. The learning curve in this business is different for everyone. Some people catch on to it right away while it takes others quite some time to "*get it*".

I encourage you to take as much time as you need to learn everything you need to know for the style of trading or investing you wish to do and build your trading plan around that style. There is a lot to know to be successful in this business and the more you can know in advance *the higher the probability* of you having a positive financial outcome from working in the live market. Anything else is not acceptable.

Right now, your *main concern* should be to gather all the pertinent information you can to decide if the financial market industry is a good fit for you. This book offers information to give you a starting point for further exploration.

Newbie Forex Traders Bible is meant to *expedite* your learning curve which can sometimes be long and *costly*. I spent 5 years teaching myself and learning how to trade and invest. As I said, you can Google *this* or *that* information however it would take you *many years* to learn what I am going to tell you in this book before you could invest any of your hard earned real money in the live markets and have a chance making real money.

Here's a thought for you to ponder. If you are studying the same information and the same books that everyone else is then don't you think you would have the same results as everyone else? If you are buying and selling with everyone else you are bound to make the same mistakes and have the same results. Now ask yourself *this* question. Am I in the business to make money or lose it? High probability says that if you study the same information as the sheeple of the herd you will become *one of them* and have the same trading results as them. Remember this *always*. Everyone other than *you* is your competition and you *must* develop an edge to beat them.

As has been said many times before but is worth repeating in **Newbie Forex Traders Bible** trading is *not* a get rich quick business, it is not the lottery, and it is not some magic lamp with a money genie that can make you rich with a wave of their hands. The only people getting rich quick in this business are banks and hedge funds. They use OPM (other people's money) and lots of leverage to put on huge bets that, if they lose, they really didn't lose because they aren't using their own money. Retail sheeple of the herd traders don't have that luxury.

New traders waste a lot of time and energy looking for the holy grail of trading methods and while it does exist it is not what you think and I just told you exactly what it is above. As I said the education part of the trading business adds a lot of marketing hype to what trading is when it is mostly just common sense. Most new traders are so focused on how much money they can make they don't think about how much money they *can lose* and that is a problem. Traders tend to look at trading and making money in the short term versus the long term. *Now you know how to look at it.*

As a new investor and self-directed trader you need be properly prepared

The live markets are an intimidating and brutal place for someone who starts off with the wrong information. They can be a mysterious, murky, and complicated place for the ill advised. By following the advice in this book and keep it simple and taking very slow and absorbing every detail you can have the best chance for a high probability outcome as a successful market participant. Make no mistake the market can make you *lose your mind, burn your soul, and help you to lose all your money.* Quickly!!

You will know in the first five pages of this book whether you want to pursue this business or not. There are quite a few things you have to make decisions about *before* you even begin your pursuit of education and learning and I hope to give you the right information in order for you to make the right decisions from the start.

When I give a reference I will put the web link to it and also tell you how to find more information and even how to word the search string for your search engine of choice. Doesn't matter which one you use as they all lead to the same data. I give you specific actions you can take to know what to do *BEFORE* you ever start investing or trading with real money.

Terminology and industry jargon has been kept to a minimum so that if English is not your native language you are still able to fully understand and comprehend what is being spoken about. I also tried to write it in plain, simple and clear enough language so that it can be translated into any language in the world if need be. There is a glossary of abbreviations at the end to help you with the market speak that is sometimes shortened, and also some extra tips and links to help you in your education.

The market and the business of the market are about **making money**. The markets are there for people to make money every day. You just have to go in there and get it. Once you know what you are doing and have done the proper education and training it is not that hard.

Learning the right information needed to get started is one of the most critical steps to be a successful market participant over the long term. Professional investors and traders know this and have taken all the proper education and training they needed to become successful.

The average time frame that it takes someone to go from starting with absolute *zero knowledge* and learning the business from scratch to consistently profitable on a daily basis is said to be in the neighborhood of 3-5 years. I know that's *not* what you want to hear but *it is* the harsh reality. The reason the learning curve is so long for some brand new traders is because they try to learn *everything* all at one time.

I liken doing training for day trading to driving a Formula One race car. You cannot just get in the car and drive it. You must learn *all* the technical aspects of how the car operates first. To get into this type of car without knowing what to do could cost you your life.

Another example I can give is learning to be a neurosurgeon. You can't just read some books, take a few courses perhaps, and then walk into an operating room and start doing brain surgery. It is more like 8-10 years of continuous very rigorous training and hands on application.

The same applies for learning trading. You first need to become familiar with chart reading, price action, market dynamics, supply and demand trading and how the trading platform you are using works and how to execute a position, place a stop loss order and exit order on the given platform. This list can go *on* and *on* for a long time depending on how much you want to learn. The result of *not* doing the proper preparation in *this* business though is that you lose *all* your money.

It is my hope that by releasing this book series in this way, a new investor and trader will be able to learn what they need to know. Save your time and money by engaging in the financial market education the right way, the first time.

There is an endless amount of information out there on investing and trading, however, no one breaks down the information for people who have *zero* experience. The way I am releasing the information will cut down your learning curve, should you decide to make a go of it in this business. This book gives you an excellent chance of succeeding if you take the advice and *do it the right way*.

Why a chart is a chart and price action rules – how do *you* see it?

This section is going to give you a *basic* understanding of reading a price chart, price action and few other skills you need to master right away if you wish to do set it and forget it type trading. You will learn much more in-depth chart reading skills to help you make buying and selling decisions in the live markets using your real money as you progress after reading this book and completing your education and training.

The first basic knowledge that a new investor and trader needs to learn is to how to read a price chart, read price action of the financial instruments they desire to work within, learn how to use supply and demand value areas to trade from. Mastering these skills and becoming competent at them is critical to being able to move forward and becoming consistently profitable on a daily basis.

Knowing how to read a price chart and price action can arm you with the edge you need to have the highest probability of having a positive outcome in the live markets you chose to work in. I strongly urge you to learn chart reading and price action if you want to be successful in today's fast moving markets. Reading price action on a chart properly and using supply and demand to trade is what wins in today's financial markets. You can do it however you want however trust me when I say that if you should skip a step or miss something it can/will cause you to lose some money in the live market.

A price chart is the graphical representation of how a financial instrument travels to supply and demand value areas over a set period of time. The chart shows where price action is and also where it *IS NOT*. In other words how long did price spend in a value area and how far away from the area did it travel over time before returning to that value area.

This graphical representation of price action or PA can take a few different forms. Price action can look like lines, bars, candle sticks, point and figure, etc. I use candle sticks because that is how I see PA the best. You should use what charts you see price action the best with.

There is a lot of information that candle sticks can show on the price chart besides PA however that is beyond the scope of this basic book. I encourage you to get comfortable with using candle sticks and knowing the basic formations, what they mean and are used for. There are excellent free candle stick courses online and I encourage you to use them.

Price only moves up sideways or down. It can't be that hard to learn right? It is all other information coming at an investor and trader which cause them to fumble and make mistakes. New investors and traders make mistakes because they do not take the proper time to learn how to read a price chart and the price action of the asset class they want to work in.

Learning to read a price chart properly takes some time and learning to read the price action of a specific instrument can take a long time to get to know all the nuances of the price action of that particular market. It does not happen overnight. All the information an investor or trader needs is right there on the chart in front of them they just have to train their eyes to see it.

It is also recommended that you study and learn the price action of your chosen instruments intimately in order to be able to know when the anticipated turns will occur. The signs of these turns are right there in front of your eyes on the price chart. It is your job to be able to spot them in real time and act on them accordingly to make money. You need to be able to look left to trade right. What is to the left has already happened, and while there is some useful data there, it is critical to know what will happen at the hard right edge and *when* it will happen.

Why price moves in these ways is to get to the areas we will be discussing shortly. It is only based on one thing and that is supply and demand in the market. Learning to be able to quantify and visually spot this on a price chart is most important for you to be able to make real money in the live markets every day.

There are only 5 outcomes from the 3 actions I stated above.

1. Make a lot of money 2. Make a little money. 3. Breakeven 4. Lose a little money 5. Lose A LOT OF MONEY!! I shout that because it's important. You need to learn how to do the first 4 and avoid doing number 5 although it can happen. To avoid doing number 5 you must **ALWAYS use a stop loss order**. ALWAYS!!! This will keep you from losing to much of your capital. If you do not have a SL (stop loss) on every position your account will be at risk of possibly blowing out. There is a saying in Vegas (amongst many) "if you don't have any checks left you can't sit at the table".

If you can learn to do numbers 1-4 above and not do the very dreaded number 5 you can make a very nice living investing and trading the any of the live markets.

Other than knowing that PA only goes up, down and sideways and using candle sticks to see this PA on the price charts it is very basic and really all you need to know. Traders and investors often make it very hard on themselves by trying to digest too much information (TMI). This only leads to losing money and is not recommended.

The human brain can only process so much information at one time. If you keep it simple that's what it will be. Don't over think it. I strongly encourage you to keep this fact as part of your trading and investing plan as it will serve you well for the rest of your career in your investing and trading business.

The other main thing you need to be able to read on the price chart is where the unfilled orders of the smart money reside in the live market. You need to be able to see this at a glance then quantify it and use the information to make a decision whether you would like to enter the market where the smart money are entering the market and be a participant along with them.

Everything you need to know is right on the price chart you are looking at every day. Once you know what to look for and learn to see it in real time *you're good*. Learn to read price action on a Forex chart, a futures chart (or any chart), and that will be 95% of what you need to know right there. It can be the other 5% is where there are some issues.

What do you think moves price action in the market from one value area to another? Filled orders or unfilled orders? If you don't know it's OK I am going to tell you right now in this book. It's the unfilled orders of the smart money that do it.

I am also going to tell you how to see them on a price chart in real time and how to take advantage of those whose orders they are. To see them you are looking for mostly areas where price is in out of balance and the signs of this are usually smaller bodied candles with barley any price action or volume in them, which is just the opposite of what is taught in all the books and trading courses. Why do you think that is?

Once you learn to see these value areas and quantify them in real time you will be able to invest in any asset class in any time frame, you will also be able to have the confidence to set it and forget it. This is the most robust method of investing and trading there is today and has been this way since the beginning of time. Every new trader thinks they need some magic method or indicator and they are sadly mistaken.

Price action you see on the charts in front of you is a graphic representation of what has already happened. What happened you ask? Orders were filled and that is what you see in the cool looking candles on the chart. It's what has *not* happened yet at the hard right edge of the chart that is the most important thing to need to be able to learn to see and read on the price chart. It's is the unfilled orders of the banks and institutional players, dark pool players, and where they reside in the live market.

It is at these value areas where you want to put your hard earned money to work in the market and then let these big guys do all the heavy moving and shaking. They are indeed the only ones who have the power and money to move price and their unfilled orders are what does it. At areas of huge supply and demand imbalance this is where this takes place. When you see a huge spike or a big old huge green or red candle it's *them* and *them only*. Learn to see this and you can make money with them very easily.

Is this something you can do over night? *Not really*. It takes time to learn to read price action. It takes time to learn to read the price action of the instrument you want to trade regularly. How much time is up to you? The more time you spend with it the better you will get to know its nuances and how and where the orders are.

Once you can see this in *real time* you will be on your way. I can't stress enough how important this is. Choose not to learn to do this and you will for sure lose some money perhaps all of it. Make no mistake about it *there are people in the markets who are there to take all your money*.

Remember this also that when you are doing your demo trading practice, no one is on the other end of the trade your placing because the trade is not being transmitted to the live market. Don't get used to trading demo like it is some video game, *It's not* and you'll be sorry you did that and so will your real money account.

I strongly encourage you to learn the price action of your chosen instrument(s) of choice intimately and familiarize yourself with the times your market has its best movements. Knowing when the smart money liquidity providers are moving the markets you want to work in is critical so you can be there to ride along with them and make money while they are doing all the hard work. It doesn't get any better than that! *Only deploy your capital in the live market when the liquidity providers are providing liquidity.*

Some real world examples to really get you thinking

Buy low sell high

This term is funny because everyone says it however not very many retail traders actually know what it really means or how to do it. Making money in the financial markets today is really *no different* than how you make money in real life. An everyday example is when you go to the grocery store with a coupon to give you a discount on the product you desire to purchase. It's really no different in the financial market; you want to buy something on sale and get the best price you can. Buy low, sell high.

Everyone likes to get a deal right? You go to your favorite Coney restaurant and sometimes have a coupon you cut out of the paper for something on the menu that they are giving a deal on that day. Investing and trading is no different. You want to buy your instrument at the *best possible price* and sell it for the highest possible profit, hence buying at wholesale and selling at retail. You also want to take the least amount of risk to do so.

We instinctively want to get the most value for our dollar. Why then, would you want to buy when an instrument price is at its highest point in the live market? This is what retail investors and traders do every day, they wait and wait, and then before they know it the price has had a big run up and they place an order out of anxiousness, Oopsy! This is also a symptom of FOMO syndrome (fear of missing out) that *all* brand new beginners have when they first start out in this business.

The problem is that retail investors and traders are conditioned to do just the opposite of this rule. They like *to think* they can buy low and sell high, however they have learned all of the *wrong information* which tells them to do the wrong thing from trading books and/or seminars. The books, seminars, and training that retail investors and traders put themselves through are often *totally unrealistic in real world markets*. Unfortunately, this often goes unrealized until it is *too late* most of the time.

Retail investors and traders buy and sell at the worst possible moments. When the price of an instrument has had a huge move up in price the retail trader is buying at the top of the move, most of the time in a panic because they thought they missed out on making money. When the price of something has had a huge move down in price they are selling at the very bottom. They have been taught to do this from the start and *don't know any better*.

Unfortunately 97% of the sheeple of the herd retail investors and traders are conditioned in their training to do just this. Here is an example that will hopefully solidify this concept for you so you will **never** make this mistake above.

This mistake happens in everyday life as well. When you walk into Sam's Club thinking that you are buying at wholesale prices, are you? Do you *really think* that Sam's is selling to you, the retail buyer, what they bought at wholesale? That big screen TV you bought from Sam at the 'bargain' wholesale price of $1200 cost good old Sam $600 because he bought 100,000 of them. You could never afford to buy that way. Sam bought low and is selling to you at higher prices than the items were purchased for, thus, making a tidy profit from you. The same thing happens in the markets every day to the retail trader. What business do you think Wall Street is in, they are in the business to make money with money and they do it by selling what they bought at a wholesale price (low) to the novice investor and trader who are conditioned to buy high at a retail (high) price.

Smart money is total and complete experts at buying at wholesale prices in the market, and selling at retail. In other words, buying low and selling high. Sounds fairly simple right? The smart money is *tooooootally* in the business to make money, which is most of the time *yours* FYI. Make no mistake about it; they are there to empty the retail investor and traders' account.

Retail investors and traders are the 'sheeple of the herd,' as I said before. They have *no idea* that they are being led down a one way street that leads to them getting fleeced. They are the ones who are paying the smart money and the professional traders thus losing all of their own assets in the live markets every single day. *WHY?* Because they have been trained and conditioned to do so right from the very start of their time in the business by learning to buy high and sell low.

When learning the business of investing and trading. Retail investors and traders are taught unrealistic principles from the start. They are shown how to buy when what they should be doing is selling and vice versa. They are taught to buy an instrument when all the 'conditions' say it's the right time. Retail traders come rely on indicators which supposedly are to help them make trading decisions. Trust me, no kind of edge or high profits can come from using lagging indicators, **no edge = no profits**.

Unfortunately for them, the markets operate in precisely the opposite manner. Typically, they are buying at the wrong time when the price is peaking already, so they are actually buying high and after everyone else has already bought and have no one to buy behind them to pay them. They normally do this where supply outweighs demand, so price *must* go down. It is at these value areas where the smart money and professional traders are waiting to take the other side of the retail trader's *mistake trade*. Buy waiting and buying high you have no one to pay *you*. By buying low everyone else who buys *after* you pays you. As I always say, don't be the one who pays be the one who *gets* paid!

Once you to start to think like the smart money and adopt their mentality and you can see and quantify where they are selling or buying in the live market, then you can make money right along with them *instead* of paying them. If you want to be consistently profitable in your investing and trading business, you *must* accept and absorb these basic supply and demand principles *immediately.*

Learning to identify where the smart money is selling and buying on the price chart takes some time. Once you have this skill mastered, you will turn your trading around, I know I did. I had to unlearn 95% of what I had learned over the course of 5 years. However, once I learned this new skill and started investing and trading with this understanding, I became consistently profitable almost overnight. Now I laugh all the way to the bank right along with the smart money. I have honestly become one of those sharks we were talking about earlier.

If you bought this book and have *zero* experience in the markets, I would encourage you study supply and demand investing and trading right from the start of your time in this business because it is the *only method* through which a markets price moves from one value area to another. Look up supply and demand trading online at the clickable link in the extra links section at the end of the book and then watch and learn everything you possibly can about it. Become an *expert* at identifying where the smart money has their orders in the live market and then mimic their actions. Pretty soon, you will be laughing all the way to the bank as well.

Here is a trick I give the people I mentor to use. You want to get the best price in the market right? Buy low sell high as it were. Cut out a coupon (any coupon) out of the paper and tape it to the top of your trading station monitor so you can always see it. Then when it is time for you to pull the trigger look at that coupon and ask yourself "am I really buying low" "am I really selling high"? After a while you will have broken yourself of *any* bad habits, trust me.

Easiest Fastest way to more pips in Forex –
managing your money right

Do you like money? Do you like *your* money?

This section is worth its weight in gold and the
information is *priceless* for a brand new trader and
while lengthy it is worth every cent you paid for this
book. If you have zero experience or have already
started your trading business but have begun to falter
it's OK. The information I am going to give to you in this
section is the *most important information you will ever
receive in your trading career about money* so I
encourage you to really take the time to absorb it and
follow it if you would like to be a consistently profitable
market participant.

Strict money management and risk control *is essential*
to achieve long-term success in the financial markets.
The high level of leverage and margin available to
traders makes it important to manage risk exposure and
to avoid overleveraged positions. As I said earlier if you
are going to use leverage or margin you had better
learn *everything* about it and what can happen to you if
you get jammed up on a trade going bad on you. *Always
trade with a stop loss!*

If I had only 1 tip I could give brand new investors and
traders coming into the business who have zero
knowledge and have not done any research, training or
education yet, I would tell them to study money
management and risk management first *before* they

even begin to look at any other information about the investing and trading business. If you only take away one thing from reading this entire book I would tell you it should be that to study money management and risk management *first* will be the most important you have ever done for yourself as an investor and trader.

New people *do not spend nearly enough time* learning about risk management and money management and it gets them into trouble right from the start. You need to have a risk management plan to be able to be consistently profitable in investing and trading in the live markets. If you don't, you mine as well write a check to your broker for the entire balance of your capital account because you will undoubtedly lose *every bit of it* without a plan.

Being wrong in trading isn't *wrong* however *staying wrong* in trading will be *death* to your account! Your job in your investing and trading business is to be a money manager not a money maker. You get paid to take risks yes, however you have to be an expert at controlling them, the money is just a byproduct of that function. The truth of it is simple, money management wins over time, there is no other way to put it. The very first thing that a brand new trader should learn and *understand completely* is risk and money management.

All of the people I know in this business who are money makers actually do not even worry about making money. There sole focus is preserving the capital *they already have*. They manage their risk on every position at all costs and know that they can have a loser every now and then and are ok with it.

When people ask me for help getting started in the trading business one of the first things I ask them is if they have studied money management and risk management. To many times I have had people come to me for mentoring help and I ask them how much time they spent on learning money management. Most of the time, the answer I get is "what do you mean"; it never surprises me and is the response I anticipate.

If a brand new trader takes the time to learn money management in the beginning there won't be any having to go backward in the learning curve, which can get *verrrrry* expensive. Unfortunately *no one* tells new traders they need to study money management first and they are left to fill in the blanks themselves. Well now, if you have purchased this book and you are brand new to trading, you know that you need to study money management first if you don't want to lose money in the live market.

The number one thing I have people learn who come to me for help when they are first starting out is risk and money management, they don't get to learn *anything* else before this is mastered 100%. This is the one area where most new people make some of their mistakes. I find that they are quick to jump into trading their demo accounts once they have some knowledge about the mechanics of trading however they have spent *very little* or *no time at all* on learning money management. Once they start losing money right away they wonder what the heck is happening and *why* things are working like they thought.

Everyone wants to make *some* money in the live markets. That is what this business is all about however one must take the *proper steps* to make sure that they have all of the information to be able to do so in the *live* market. Without proper money management skills it is very easy to develop bad habits on the demo account which when taken with them into a live market situation *can cause serious damage* to a real money account and very quickly. These bad habits are very hard to break once they are developed and ingrained into the traders psyche.

In learning money management a new self-directed investor or trader can begin to see what their own personal risk tolerance is. You *must* know this *before* ever stepping foot in the live market with your hard earned real money. There are plenty of scenarios and formulas for risk management however what most investors and traders find out is that they will only want to lose a *set sum of money* before saying OK that's enough and close out a losing position with a loss. Part of being a winning professional trader is to learn how to lose professionally as well. You *will not* win every single position you enter, you should *also* be prepared for *that*.

Most of these professionals have what I call "smart plans" meaning their position is managed from the time it is executed in the live market until the time it closes itself out at the designated profit target. Notice I said closes *itself* out. That is because most professionals including me use an automated system to do their trading.

Money management in the live market is what it is all about not trading. You don't actually make money by trading you make money by being in the market *in* your position. If you don't have any money left you can't *be* in the market.

To succeed at trading the financial markets, you need to not only thoroughly understand position sizing, and risk amount per trade, you also need to *consistently execute* each of these aspects of money management in combination with a highly effective yet simple to understand trading strategy that uses price action in conjunction with supply and demand principles.

Learning money management requires time and attention to detail that most all new traders are not willing to do. Once you have a live position in the market you go from be a trader to a risk and money manager. The only thing you have control over once you are in the live market is how much money you *don't lose*.

Experienced successful investors and traders know that employing a rule based money management strategy is one of critical concepts of risk management. Money management for account preservation is not sexy at all and very boring to study however they are *the most important* skills in investing and trading that person in the business need to have an understanding of and to have *mastered*.

If you *cannot* fully grasp and understand the implications of money management as well as how to actually implement money management principles and techniques, you have a *very limited* chance of becoming a consistently profitable trader. Until you *completely understand* and *are comfortable with* how to have, and how to follow a money management plan I encourage you to *stay out* of the live market.

Not learning proper trade and money management – Not using stop losses and cutting losses early. You hear that a million times in your investing and trading career. Why is it then, that almost every brand new investor and trader lacks this skill? They have not taken the time to learn this very important skill from the start and it almost always causes them some account pain in the beginning.

The main reason why the professionals are so successful is because they stick to their plan no matter if they are losing money or making a lot of money. They *do not ever* deviate from their plan because they know that over a long period of time they will be consistently profitable from having done so.

These people have developed an *edge* over the sheeple of the herd and exploit them with their edge to make money from them every day. They know what mistakes the sheeple of the herd make over and over again on a daily basis and so does the smart money.

The successful investor or trader then just watches for the smart money to make their move on the sheeple of the herd and then just capitalize right along with them on their power and volume. They know that the herd does not trade with a plan and can see their errors because of it.

There is no letting a position that is in profit come back to turn into a loser due to having the stop loss already in the live market. I have entered the position *already knowing* what my stop loss amount is money wise so there is no question as to how much I will lose should the position not work out as planned. Once the profit target is hit the position automatically closes and then it is time to look for the next opportunity.

Profitable investors and traders know they can make consistent profits *over time* and do not look to make all their money on one or two big positions. They realize and accept they will have a higher probability of having a positive outcome over *many successful outcomes* in the market versus just a few. They only are looking for the lowest risk highest reward positions and will just **wait** until the opportunity arises. When the opportunity *does* come they are decisive and take *immediate* action. Once the action has completed they look for the next one.

Being decisive to smooth your equity curve and managing risk effectively are the skills which should be focused on learning first *versus* last and unfortunately most losing retail investors and traders don't realize this **until it is too late**. This is what makes consistently profitable investors and traders different than unprofitable investors and traders.

Having a set plan and also having it automated so your profit target and stop loss are deployed when your position is executed in the live market is another way to avoid making money mistakes. As I said before, the only thing you have control of once you are in the live market is how much money you *don't lose*. By doing it this way and having it automated you can take out some of the stress involved when your real money is working in the live market.

A money management plan for the type of trading you are doing should be tailored to what *your* risk appetite is *not* anyone else's. Trading is a very personal business and what works for one trader will *not* work for another. Another way to make your money management plan your own is to compose it to what market you are working and also what time frame you are working in that market.

Your plan should take into account the volatility of the market, time of day you are trading, how many lots or contracts you are trading with. Most successful traders in the market have this information incorporated into their plan and that is what makes them so successful.

The first and foremost thing about money management is to have a plan and then *actually* use it. To many times traders will compose a money management plan, go in the live market, get into some trouble on a position and the plan goes *out the window*. Unfortunately so does *large amounts* of their risk capital most of the time.

I tell brand new traders what they will find that works for them the best is the *most simple* money management strategy that they can come up with. They will not know for sure how successful it will be, however that is better than to not have anything in place and doing nothing. The only people I know who make money every day in the markets are the people who have great money management skills, and are well capitalized for the type investing and trading they do. To do it any other way invites financial disaster and risk of ruin. Don't be that trader!

Once you have studied risk management and then apply it to how you want to invest and trade you can begin to have some success *as long as* you stick to your money management plan and ***never*** deviate from it. This is where most retail traders get themselves into trouble and cause themselves to lose money. They will set a stop loss and then when price action approaches the stop they will adjust it or take it out altogether. **BAD IDEA!** Once your stop loss is in the market you should *never move it.*

Risk in investing and trading is *unavoidable* however with the proper training and a good sound plan can be diminished when the plan is followed. Risk is also diminished over time when the investor and trader gains more knowledge as to how much appetite for risk they really have. Without this knowledge the investor or trade cannot gain an understanding or get the experience and competence to make consistent profits.

When you make the decision to go live with real money, that's when it gets serious and very real for you. You are now in competition with the big boys, who have billions of dollars to play with and have the best super computer technology in the world and code slinging geeks to tell the computer what to see and what trades to execute.

You absolutely need to have a competitive edge in the markets, and you must have it *before* you do anything in the live markets with real money. I will have some other books out that detail how to develop your edge for making money in today's live markets, I encourage you to read them all as soon as they come out if you are in this business to make money. If you run with the 'sheeple of the herd' you can be assured to *not have any edge* so don't, they all study the same information and are all programmed the same way to lose money repeatedly.

To be consistently profitable over the long term one must consider capital preservation their number one rule. *To be successful in this business it cannot be any other way.* It takes money to make money in the financial markets and *once your money is gone it is gone*. This is why I tell clients they *must* study risk and money management *first* and *foremost*.

The moment your deploy capital in the live market you go from being an investor or day trader to a risk and money manager. You have *already* determined the probabilities of having a positive outcome on a position before you took it. Now all there is to do is sit back and let the market pay you by managing your risk on the position. Once you have your money management plan and rules in place it is critical that you be disciplined to follow the plan and all the rules at all costs. It is best to have them written out in a word document or a spread sheet and kept right by you at your work station at all times for reference if you need to.

All professional investors and traders I know will say the same thing if asked what is the number one thing they consider to be important in their business that is *capital preservation*. If you lose all your money in the market you can't *be* in the market.

You don't need to be "*in there*" all the time. I only deploy my capital in the live market when I am 100% sure of what I want to do *before* I do it. I only have to win around 40% of the time to make a nice return from the live market. I am only looking for the lowest risk, highest reward, and highest probability opportunities. I swing and position trade so I do not have to take action that often however when I do everything is I do is *predetermined* by my plan criteria.

A trick I have traders I help out use is to set their demo account balance to whatever amount they think they will be going to capitalize their real money account with, this way they will know *right off* if they can work in the live market with that amount of capital or not.

I did not choose to do that and the first time I went in the live futures market and as I said, I promptly lost two thousand dollars. I got back out and studied more. I went back in the live market again and lost *another* two thousand dollars. Now I am down a total of four thousand dollars real money and scratching my head going dude WTF.

The reason I had lost money is because I did not have any money management skills developed. What I just said I lost is the perfect example of that. The live market *is not* the place to be if you have not done your proper education. There are sharks with fully loaded revolvers in the market waiting for you.

I tell new people that what they are going to find is that what is going to work for them in the long run in their own business and makes money for them is a combination of things they have learned from others and on their own. They put it all together and all of the sudden they have something going and an edge that is making them money on a consistent basis. The only thing that matters in the live market is what works for *you* and makes *you* money. *Once you have found your edge never ever share it!*

Risk management should be very important to you as a trader if you want to be consistently profitable. You always need to be thinking in terms of capital preservation and not worried as much about capital appreciation. If your plan is solid, the money will come on its own if you are following your rule based plan.

Your job as a trader is not to make money your job is to *manage* the money you *already have* so you can make more. You can't sit at the table if you don't have any checks as they say in Vegas.

Even if you were careless and lost only 50% of your capital you would still need to make 100% to get all your money back. It is possible to do this albeit very hard, and *not likely*, especially for the retail sheeple of the herd. Once they begin to lose money they will start to jump around to different asset classes and systems, this only compounds their problems.

All the trading books (including mine), say that you should not ever risk more than 1 – 2% of available trading capital on any given day trade. On Swing trades, this number may be 3 – 5% of their trading capital. You will have a maximum dollar amount you can lose on any trading day, and **you will cease trading immediately when that number is hit**. What this number is to you depends on your account size. *You should never trade more than you are willing to lose*. The larger your account is *the less* you should be using as risk. On some of my accounts I use .025%.

If you set your daily goal at $600 dollars and are risking $200 on a trade and are stopped out 3 times then **you are done** for that trading day. Turn your charts off and go have a good day. The market will be there waiting for you the next time.

Trading and thinking like a consistently profitable trader will allow your trading to improve enormously and the profits will come much easier as you learn to control your risk and let the profits take care of themselves. Always using a SL that's within your comfort level as far as risk goes. You get paid to take risk. So take risk! But also be a money manager. Everyone I know in this business has the goal of having their SL *as close to their entry* as possible thus having the lowest amount of risk possible. Experienced traders control risk, inexperienced traders just chase money. **You will not have a 100 % success rate**... if you win 51 % and lose 49 % you just need to make a nice living out of the 2 % difference.

The capital one starts their business with should be capital that is *disposable*. Meaning that if all the capital happened to be lost to the markets the investor or trader would not be hurt by the loss *in any way*. I have clients I mentor do that visualization I was talking about earlier in this book. I have them think about throwing their starting capital into their barbeque and turning it on and watching their money burning up in flames and smoke.

It sounds harsh I know, however *the reality of it is* that when a new investor or trader who has entered the business is not using a rules based plan, has not done the proper education and training and learned what they need to know to take only high probability positions that will give the highest reward and have the lowest risk the outcome is virtually almost always the same. Flames and smoke!

Once you have your money management plan and rules in place it is *critical* that you be disciplined, follow the plan and all the rules at all costs. It is best to have them written out in a word document or a spread sheet and kept right by you at your work station at all times for reference.

Having a set plan and also having your profit target and stop loss be deployed when your position is executed in the live market is another way to avoid making mistakes. As I said before the only thing you have control of once you are in the live market is how much money you *don't lose*. By doing it this way you can take out some of the stress involved when your real money is working in the live market.

There is also plenty of information on risk management and money management online. I would tell you to figure out *what type* of trader you want to be and to figure out what your money goals are first and then tailor your money management plan to the goals you set for yourself. Learn the *right* information the *right way* from the *first* day and you should have *no problems*.

Protecting their capital is what professional trader's do most however they also take great steps to protect the amount of unrealized profit that becomes part of the total equity of his account. To the experienced professional protecting profits is just as important as protecting themselves and limiting losses.

Having a "smart plan" should be the goal of every futures trading business. Smart money management should be a part of every trading strategy and it is something that I really stress all the time to new traders who come to me for help. I tell them to just *stay out* of the live market until they have a plan composed that they know works for them that is suited for their personality type and also the type trading which they desire to do.

Manage your risk capital with a good risk management profile, and you will be in the markets for as long as you want to be in them. ***Any other scenario is not acceptable***. You can do a search for the following to get more information: Trading risk management, money management in day trading, risk of ruin.

If you haven't mastered money management I strongly encourage you to *stay out* of the live markets until you do. To really succeed at trading the financial markets, you need to not only <u>thoroughly</u> understand risk reward, position sizing, and risk amount per trade, you also need to consistently execute each of these aspects of money management in combination with a highly effective yet simple to understand trading strategy like price action and supply and demand principles. You can do all the scans you want however until you master money management those scans *won't help you*.

The best principle in risk management can be stated in three words. *"**Use a stop**"*! No one, *especially* a brand new trader or investor can be prepared enough for the *volatility* and *brutality* of the live market. It is fine to practice on a demo account to learn your software platform for entries and exits however it is completely another thing to be able to do it in a live market environment with the best market participants in the world who are trying to take your money. *Keep it simple, be prepared, have a plan and watch your money and you can't go wrong.*

As a newbie your ego is not your amigo

Professional traders have a secret weapon that makes them successful. What is it you may be asking? They know what their limitations are and *never exceed them*. It is honestly that simple. I won't lie to you and tell you that they all knew this right from the start, *no one does*. It takes quite some time to know what one's risk tolerance is for using their hard earned real money in the live markets.

As a brand new beginner it is imperative that you have your self under control *before* you ever step foot in the live market and execute a position with your hard earned real money. Trading psychology in financial market investing and trading is very important and is something that new traders do not understand and how *critical* it is to their success.

People getting into this business who are brand new fail to develop the needed mental toughness to succeed in the markets. It is no game in there, and there are people who will walk over the wreckage of your account to get paid. Make no mistake; it takes mental toughness to do this business and *you* must develop it.

Being a consistently profitable investor and trader means *many* things. It means knowing when to be decisive and take action. It also means knowing when *not* to trade. Professionals develop a thick skin and know when something is *not* a good deal. Once you develop these skills you will know when to just "stay out". You do not have to *"be in"* the market all the time to make some money.

It takes a long time to get to this level of psychological toughness. Most new people who come into this business have unrealistic expectations on what they will be able to pull out of the market on a daily basis. We *have all* been there though. Most professionals who are at the level of consistency of making money on a daily basis if they are day traders have accepted that the market will only give out so much and they are good with that.

That should be a huge clue, however because people think this is a get rich quick business when they first get into it and they think that they can learn a few chart patterns and some price action and then can go into the live make and make jet fuel money. New traders are buying Ferrari's and Gulfstream 650's before ever making a live trade with real money.

There are many things involved in financial market trading that can cause emotional swings that can affect your trading decisions. Lack of self-control in the markets leads to stress, anxiety and ultimately money loss. No one wants that however most new traders coming into the business are looking for instant gratification and quick money. This leads to a lot of *very bad* decisions and self-sabotage in new traders and it can get *verrrrry* ugly!

Having your head on straight and your psychology in order is something you *must* master *before* you *ever* step foot into the live market with your hard earned real money. Unfortunately this is one of the biggest mistakes brand new traders make when they first enter the business, and was mentioned in the mistakes brand new traders make chapter, I encourage you to re-read that entire chapter if need be.

The professional trader knows that becoming emotional over a position can be the cause of their losing money and they *avoid losing their money like it is the plague.* I know for me I would rather eat broken glass and wash it down with gasoline or light myself on fire than lose money back to the market so I just turn everything off. How do I do that? It's not easy and takes *a long time* to master. I trade like I am in a fugue state. I am here by myself in my office with zero distractions other than my trusted companion Angel my cat he's always on me about clicking the mouse too much.

You must *master* your own psychology. Having structure and discipline are traits of the most successful investors and traders. Having these two traits among others are critical to being a professional self-directed investor and trader. Without them it will be *very hard* to become consistently profitable on a daily basis. All investors and traders who are successful have the same traits when it comes to working in the live markets. They know that there is a huge different between being emotional *and just plain stupid* about their investing and trading in the markets.

Too many times I see brand new traders coming in thinking they can outsmart the market, guess what *you can't*. You are the one who is going to get FUBAR. This part of this book will serve as a guide for the brand new investor and trader with *zero experience* and give you a starting point as to what to study and where to go to get more information on trading psychology. There are plenty of articles out there on trading psychology and I encourage you to read the ones that may pertain to any issues *you* may think *you* have before beginning in this business.

One thing I can tell you that is an **absolute** about the live market is that as I said, there are people in there who will walk over dead bodies *to get paid and make money* and you can bet they would walk over yours to get you to pay them *rest assured*. You must learn to have a "kill everyone" mentality when working in the live markets. You must be able to be decisive and have zero fear and the confidence in your skills to know you will make the right decision at the right time and always follow your plan. They will carve your account up like it is a Thanksgiving turkey and not break a sweat, *they eat money*.

By now if you have read *this* far, this book might be *scaring the crap out of you*. That is probably a good thing. If you are brand new and want to really *do* this business and *are not just playing around.*

Here are some things to ask yourself before you begin your investing and trading education and training. Am I the type of individual who is impulsive, tend to worry a lot? Can I remain calm in very tense circumstances? Can I be decisive when it comes time to make a hard decision? Do I have the ability to follow rules and follow a plan of action? Can I solve complex problems while under pressure?

If you can answer these questions **honestly** to yourself you may have a good chance at becoming a successful investor and trader. If you are *not* able to be truthful with yourself I will be brutally honest with you here, perhaps it might be best to look at another profession.

You must build a rock solid foundation of principles to work from in investing and trading and a psychological base is no different than the trading base. You must have it from the beginning to become successful; you must develop structure and discipline that is *unbending.*

Having structure and discipline are traits of the most successful investors and traders. Having these two traits among others are critical to being a professional self-directed investor and trader. Without them it will be *very hard* to become consistently profitable on a daily basis.

Investors and traders *must* be able to keep their emotions in balance when doing this business. The *worst thing* traders can do is to become emotional over a position. When a position is going against them, they can get stressed, knowing they can lose money. Losing money is part of the cost of doing business, and it is a *known fact*, so *there is no reason* to become stressed over it. Wasn't it Gordon Gekko that said "Relax pal, first lesson in business is don't get emotional about stocks - it clouds your judgment." I couldn't have said it better myself!

Professional traders don't *let* emotions cloud their judgment and rattle them. Despite the stress and pressure that come with their work, they can remain focused and execute their rule based plan without hesitation. They have mental and emotional toughness.

It's this kind of motivation, mental toughness and highly competitive by nature as well as an inner driving force to overcome competition that fuels the best traders to go the extra mile to achieve their goals. You have to be willing to have a "kill everyone" mentality to work in the live markets. Professional traders know that there are people in the live markets who will walk over dead bodies to get paid and have no qualms about following the smart money down that path of least resistance everyone is always talking about.

Successful traders know their own trading personality profile, they know what makes them tick (no pun intended). They all have developed all the personality traits needed to be a consistently profitable market participant over the long term. They develop habit patterns such as having a morning routine that they do religiously every day before trading. I talked about them at length earlier in the book so now might be a good time to re-read those habits and make a note to start developing them.

When clients come to me for mentoring one of the first things I ask them is if they have looked inside themselves, *the only place a trader becomes successful from is within*. A mentor or a trading coach can only help a new investor or trader so much. New aspiring investors and traders must look within themselves and figure out what they need to do to enhance and perfect their performance in the live market.

I tell all new investors and traders they must have their emotions under control *before* they ever set foot in the live markets and put their hard earned money to work. It is one thing to learn how to execute your trading plan on a demo account to learn how the platform you will be utilizing to place your positions in the live market. It is entirely another thing to do it in a live market environment with the best market participants in the world. I suggest moving into the live market as soon as possible on a micro account in order to experience the psychology of live market environment trading and the feelings that go along with using real money to work with, *especially if you're losing*. As I said, you can be wrong you just can't **stay** wrong.

Take some small real money positions and always use a stop loss and profit target. If you use an ATM strategy that places the stop and the profit target at the time the position order is placed in the live market, there should be nothing to do but sit back and let the market do all the work, you can be strictly *hands off*.

The less you have to do while in a live position, the better off you are. There is no stress involved in letting the market do all the work for you. If a position goes against you, then you have a possibility of losing money. If you already realize this before you enter the market, then again I will say, there should be no stress or anxiety about it.

When readying yourself to move into the live markets with real money you should have overcome all of the following issues. Fear of success as it will hold you back from achieving consistency and being indecisive when making a trade decision. If you are following your plan this should not be an issue at all. You should have overcome *all* barriers to making mistakes while executing your plan.

You are not hesitant **at all** and can execute a position *without any emotion* at all and then follow through for the final outcome *good* or *bad*. You have removed *all* stressors from your trading environment (no kids, no pets, **NO WIFE**). You are now committed to becoming a consistently profitable market participant and know that you are able to go in to the live market with zero fear and know that there will be losses at times and are ok with that.

Losing money is part of the cost of doing business, and it is a *known fact,* so there is no reason to become stressed over it. It is what it is, and is **going to happen** at some point the question is *how much* you lose. Quite honestly that *is* the only thing you have control of once your capital is deployed in the live market.

There is also a lot of fear involved in trading. When traders make a mistake in their analysis, which causes them to take a loss, they can develop a fear of being wrong all the time. This can psychologically prevent them from "pulling the trigger" when they need to. This is all the more reason to trade with a plan and stick to in *good* times and *bad.*

The flip side of that is that traders will not let a position go to its profit target and thus cannot realize the full profit potential of the position and cause themselves not to make as much money as they could have. They close the position out early before the profit target is hit for fear of losing the gains they already have in the position. If you have analyzed your supply and demand value areas properly this should not be an issue and your profit margin *should already be known*.

The worst thing traders can do is grudge trade or impulse trade. They think that they have to get back at the market due to having a loss. What they *should* do is take a break and walk away, get some air, have something to eat, or whatever. Then go back and evaluate what happened with a clear perspective. Unfortunately, this is hardly the case, and often traders go *right back* into the markets and continue to lose money. The market *doesn't care* if you take a loss; however, *you* should!

The day you "pull the trigger" and go from your demo account to your real live trading account your whole world is going to change including your emotions. It did for all of us who have made it and it will for you as well. You *will* have to do it however the better prepared you have made yourself for the outcomes the better you will do from the onset of your live market activity.

I have a great idea what price is doing and where price action is going to go before it goes there with a high degree of certainty from quantifying the price action of the asset I am working in. I do this the same way every time without deviation or hesitation. When the chart tells me the information I need to know for entry I act on it with unwavering action.

In this section I will leave you with this. Check your ego at the door please it doesn't belong in the live markets. The thing I am saying here is that in live market trading you need to check your ego at the door when the opening bell sounds. In the live financial markets your ego is not your amigo! There is a line in a song that comes to mind here. "Check yourself before you wreck yourself".

To trade like a machine a trader must be well prepared at the beginning of every trading day. This can only come from paying attention to detail, mastering a strategy and focusing on execution. Also, knowing who you are trading against is critical. If you understand, and can identify the human emotions of fear and greed of the sheeple of the herd on a price chart you can make these emotions work for you instead of against you. Putting all this together is what will make you a world class trader.

You can do a simple search for "trading psychology" online and do more research as to what you need to know and how you can overcome any issues you may have *before* making any costly mistakes. *This is what it takes to become a professional in this business.*

The importance of choosing the right trading tools as your method – supply and demand

There will not be anything in this section I will talk about other than supply and demand, and you will find out how to learn how to use these principles in the live markets to make some real money every day. I do not listen to news, I do not use *any* indicators, and there is no fancy system or method you have to learn. It's simple price action, supply and demand, along with training your eyes to see where unfilled smart money orders reside at in the live market. That's it!

Use price action with supply and demand to have a lethal double whammy edge over the sheeple of the herd who have all studied the wrong information from the start on day one, and have been taught unrealistic information that will not help them in any way in the live market. Use price action with supply and demand with sound money management and a detailed trading plan for whatever instruments you desire to work in and there should be no reason you cannot make *some* money every day in the live market once you have studied and prepared yourself properly.

My hope from this part of this book is that you understand how important it is to have a competitive edge when putting your hard earned money at risk in the markets. Each day, the wealth from trader accounts is transferred from those without an edge into the accounts of those who have developed that all needed important winning edge.

The key to success when trading the live markets with supply and demand comes down to a few things: What is the object of supply and demand trading? To gain the ability to objectively quantify bank and institution demand and supply on a price chart, knowing what a supply and demand imbalance looks like and how to take advantage of that opportunity with objective and mechanical rules. Seems simple right?

To be a successful market speculator and investor you must be equipped with the proper tools and information from the start of your trading and investing business. Price action and the use of supply and demand principles to make trading and investment decisions *are* those tools. You don't need to care where the price is going to be ten years from *now*; you need to know about where price is _right_ now.

You don't need any of the latest fad trading systems that the gurus are touting. All you need are the time tested principles of supply and demand. Combine that with the price action of your chosen instrument and you have all the edge you need over the sheeple of the herd.

I purposely do not include any charts, tables, or formulas in this book. No mathematical equations to memorize. I'll tell you why. This book is not about learning any particular method or system. It is about learning how to get the right start on your new business the right way the first time. It is about getting the right information from day one. It is my intent for you the reader to be able to do just that. *READ.*

I would like for you to be able to actually absorb what you are reading as this information will be some of the *most important information you read in your life* when it comes to what you need to know to be successful in the live markets with your hard earned real money. I want nothing but the best outcome for you so I owe it to you to give you best information I can.

OK traders the next place you need to go and the next thing you need to start to grasp is basics and foundation then application of these supply and demand principles in the live markets. You can do a search online for a supply and demand foundation and application course. I encourage you to watch every video and read every article and book you can on this style of investing and trading you can get your hands on.

Here is a good start for you brand new investors and traders looking to understand supply and demand dynamics and use it to invest and trade in the live markets of today. It is economics 101 pretty much. You should learn it though if you want to know and understand what really makes price do what it does in the live market because it is this and nothing else.

So that I do not sound redundant in my explanations after we move on from this point I will direct you to go here: http://www.investopedia.com/university/economics/economics3.asp for an explanation of the dynamics of supply and demand which will from this point be the only thing mentioned as far as a way of investing and trading is concerned in the live market.

Supply and demand is not rocket science and no one owns it, or has a patent on it and *anyone* can learn it. It is a simple market principle that has been in existence since there was a market. It will always be the same principle till there is no more market which will be the end of days.

You do not have to be a math wizard to get it and you do not have to memorize any formulas or math equations. It is just a simple yet powerful principle that when armed with its knowledge and the knowledge of the price action of your chosen instrument of choice you can have a serious winning edge which will give you the highest probability of having a positive outcome on being a market participant.

It all builds off of this basic principle of supply and demand right here so I encourage you to take your time and absorb it a little at a time. You will see that supply and demand investing and trading works on all asset classes on any time frame, it is a robust and repeatable process in *any* market. It does not matter if you are trading equities, Forex futures, grains or *kittens* and *puppies* for that matter. You just have to pick what TF (time frame) you like and what market(s) you want to invest in or trade and what your comfort level of risk is in those markets, it is fairly simple once you have it down pat.

Everything you see on the chart to the left has already taken place hence why all indicators except price action are lagging and of no use to a professional trader. The *ONLY* thing that matters is where those unfilled orders are resting in the market because *THAT* is where PA goes to and takes off from. The only *other* thing that matters is how much time price spent there at that price level. Learn how to read PA in this manner and you will have a high probability of making money every single day. Combine that with supply and demand dynamics and it will be all you ever have to know to make money in the live markets the rest of your natural life.

You do not need to over think *anything* in supply and demand (S&D) trading. It is very simple, the simplest in fact. I had to unlearn 95% of what I had already studied before I became consistently profitable on a daily basis in the markets. My goal is to save you brand new traders and investors who are new and wanting to learn trading a lot of time and cut down your learning curve so you can be on your way to making real money in the live markets every day. How fast you "*get it*" is up to you.

Supply and demand value areas on a price chart represent *ALL* buyers and sellers in the world who are in the live market you are looking at that time and thus it is very easy to quantify were the unfilled orders reside in the live market. As I have stated all you need to do is train your eyes to spot these value areas on the price chart you are analyzing and then make a decision whether you would like to become a market participant as well.

Mostly all of the professional traders I associate with have in the very high thousands of hours of screen time to get good at seeing and opening positions from supply and demand value areas on charts. Hopefully you will get good at it as well and become well off by doing so. The amount of screen time needed to be able to go in the live market and make real money is said to be 10,000 or more hours. Hopefully this book will help get you started and *cut down* that amount of learning curve time.

It is your job to practice to get good at recognizing the value areas. You will need to do it over and over and over again until it becomes second nature for you to spot, quantify and execute a position from these value areas *without hesitation*. As soon as you have learned and have the experience you can open positions from them in the live real markets with real money with confidence and *zero fear*.

What you are looking for is the way PA leaves the certain area which is said to be a supply or demand value area. This value area is also sometimes called a base or PA can be said to be basing. This is that sideways price action I was talking about earlier.

This huge move is normally seen as a large expanded range candle (ERC) or a bunch of them. Does not matter what color you make your candles and I suggest you just have them the same color as the color of the candles will make no difference as to what data the candle is telling you. All that matters is that you understand and become an expert at what to see, quantify it and where it is happening. When PA comes back and revisits this value area again in the future is when you want to be there waiting with your resting order in the live market.

Remember this: first come first served. Which means if your order is already there resting in the live market in the queue you have a high probability of being filled right away verses adding your order and having to wait in line with all the other orders just going in.

The way PA leaves the supply and demand value areas is also the way in tends to return to it. Meaning PA can blast back into the area with a nice big ERC or if it left the value area slowly it can meander its way back. Another way PA can leave a value area is by gapping up or down. What PA is coming back to this value area for is to fill more of the unfilled orders which were left there when price became out of balance the first time it was at this area.

To identify a demand/supply value area: 1. Look at current PA on the chart, 2. Look down and left OR up and left to locate a very strong rally in current PA. Huge candle body's work best or a gap away from it and be an indication of how strong PA is in that value area. Look for the origin of the move, what was the last price the banks were willing to sell at? Is value area fresh? Was there a strong move from this area previously? Draw line on top of basing candle and the lower line on the lowest low of the wicks. The move away from this value area to the furthest point away is the initial profit margin for the next trade op. Move should be 2-3 times the size of the value area for the most profitable trade op. Watch for how far PA penetrates into the value area on the first retracement to the value area. If PA does not quite reach the value area there may be more unfilled orders left at the value area and PA could come back here to fill more orders.

Once PA trades thru a value area and bases (4-6

candles) it becomes a new demand/supply value area. 1st retrace back to this value area is the *highest probability* of a trade working out. 2nd or 3rd retest, and the probability of the trade working out decreases each time PA retests that value area.

Watch for PA to turn on a lower time frame chart at a higher time frame S&D value area, this is the *only* place that a turn in current PA is likely to take place. When trend is changing look at the higher time frame to see *where* the previous value area was and PA should turn there on the lower TF chart. Can also watch for divergence on the indicator *if using one*, it will appear at supply or at demand.

When PA gets to a level that has been touched previously look for an reversal candle such as an engulfing , doji, shooting star with tall wick to the high/low side. Some unfilled orders where perhaps left there and Pa could turn again. After 3 touches watch for PA to trade thru the level and move higher/lower to the next value area. When PA is in a range, oscillators could perhaps be used to go between S&D value areas.

Mistakes traders make in spotting levels: 1. Not quantifying where PA is in regards to the bigger picture TF, 2. Not choosing fresh value areas, 3. Not making sure there is a profit margin to the next opposing value area.

What matters most is that we see where the smart money is deploying their assets and what best pricing they are looking for. We want to get it at what price they get it for. Believe your eyes and not your brains. It's the smart money's ginormous footprints that they leave all over our charts that really matter. It is their tracks in the market that you are looking for on your price chart in the price action of your chosen instrument. They are easy to spot once you know what you are looking for.

Once you are armed with this knowledge it does not matter what you are investing in or trading. These signals I am telling you to see are the only thing that moves price action on a chart. Any chart. Even kittens and puppies if you trade them! If you keep it simple from the start of your learning and education those skills will follow you into the live markets and be beneficial to you in making real money every day.

That's the beauty of it this method. It works on *all* liquid markets and on *any* time frame you choose to look at it on. I encourage you to work on daily charts because that is what the smart money uses. Once you can see the value areas on the daily chart you can see them on any time frame. That's what makes this method so lethal. It's the combination of price action and supply and demand value areas. *That is what wins in today's markets.*

Learn to see unfilled orders on a price chart and the PA of your preferred instrument to trade and you are home. No fancy news, no indicators, just PA and what makes the market do what it does, supply and demand. It's *THE* only thing that makes the market move.

Simple really, however traders tend to make things hard on themselves and cause a lot account pain because of it. Don't be *that* investor or trader. People just think this is a get rich quick business. It's precisely the opposite unless you are a bank or hedge fund and you are using leverage and OPM (other people's money) or a combination of both.

In S&D it's all about setting your position order and then just *waiting* and letting PA come to you. It's just a waiting game at that point. If you get filled there then you are in the market with everything already there. *IF* you do not get filled then you just cancel the order and reassess PA and look for the next signal and opportunity.

The thing about supply and demand style trading is that you either have to be there when PA reaches where you need it to be *OR* have a resting limit order in the market for when it does. That is going to take some getting used to. The whole position order needs to go in at the same time on a trade like that. Stop loss and profit target need to go in with the trade *especially the stop loss*.

If you know how to build out the chart properly you should in fact have an idea where and when PA will get to where you need it be to capitalize on it. You can make big money with the smart money not withstanding HFT's, Algo or AMM. You can't fight that in any way nor should you even try to. Hopefully you are on the right side of it and PA can sail right to your PT on the smart money's volume.

If you are still having trouble seeing the value areas I encourage you to go back and analyze why? Ask yourself these questions. Have you looked back far enough left? Are you using multiple time frames (MTF) to do analysis? Does it help you to understand how to look for and evaluate PA on higher time frame (HTF) charts and how get the curve as well? Look in your journal and analyze what you have done previously that worked and did not. Then just do what *did* work for you over and over and over again!

It is critical that you train your eyes to recognize these areas to acquire your positions from. This is where price is in balance for the moment. The way PA leaves this value area is a key piece of data for you to use in your analysis of any position you may be thinking of taking in the live market with real money. PA will normally leave a value area when it is out of balance with a huge move in PA.

What criteria do you look for when identifying a supply

and demand value area? You're probably asking what makes a supply and demand value area *better* or *worse* than another S&D value area and what criteria is used to determine those issues.? The most important two are how long has time spent at that level and is that level original? How do you define a supply or demand level *before* the fact? Before it is tested or broken through? Look left *as far as you need to* too find out if price has been to that area before. This is the difference between telling if it is a retest of a previous supply/demand level or making a pivot and a support/resistance level.

When does an S&D value area become invalid? An excellent explanation of when a supply or demand level becomes invalid is once PA breaks through and closes above or below the tested level, it is invalid. This is because all orders that were left at that level have been absorbed, thus the candle can close above the value area.

What happens, when a value area is NOT original and PA has been back to it one or more times? Chances are PA will trade through the value area because all of the previous orders that resided there have been filled and/or absorbed. When PA goes to a value area and bounces off 1 or more time orders are being filled and depleted and thus used up so when PA returns back there again it can slice right through the value area and move up/down to the next area of orders.

When PA turns at a value area there will be few candles and low volume, NOT many candles and high volume. Most traders are taught to look for a volume spike and/or many candles and retests of an area for confirmation. By the time they have their confirmation PA has *ALREADY* turned and is moving away and taking the probability of success of a positive outcome on a trade with it, and is also *increasing* the risk.

For me it is all about the value areas. As long I see them right, I make money every day as long as I don't stay long too long. LOL I still draw S&R lines and use TL as well however the trade decisions are based around what PA does at those S&D value areas and if the criteria of the set up meet my rules for entry. If you are more visual then by all means draw some TL or use whatever you like, *do whatever it takes*.

That is how I make money in the live markets every day. I just look for where the smart money have their resting orders and then wait for the retail sheeple of the herd to make their mistakes and buy or sell to or from them and then follow the smart money to where they are going to next. You don't need an MBA degree from a big fancy Ivy League college for that! Combine price action with supply and demand investing and trading and you have an edge over the retail sheeple of the herd.

My hope from this part of this book is that you understand how important it is to have a competitive edge when putting your hard earned money at risk in the markets. Each day, the wealth from trader accounts is transferred from those without an edge into the accounts of those who have developed that all needed important winning edge. *Which one do you want to be?*

The key to success when trading with an edge in the live markets with supply and demand comes down to a few things: What is the object of supply and demand trading? To gain the ability to objectively quantify bank and institution demand and supply on a price chart, knowing what a supply and demand imbalance looks like and how to take advantage of that opportunity with objective and mechanical rules. Seems simple right?

I recommend learning a method of investing and trading that can be used over *all* asset classes and on *any* time frame. The only method I found that does this and works in the live market, because that is what the live markets work on, is supply and demand. I combined that with the price action of the instruments I work in, and it has become a lethal money making combination and what *my* method is based to give me my own winning edge. *Are you ready to get yours?*

The only newbie beginner rule based plan chapter you'll ever need to read

Listen up now newbie because this is one of the biggest mistakes new self-directed traders make is what is being talked about in this chapter. You don't need a hopium pill or a rosary when you go into the live market with the sharks; *you need a freakin rule based plan*.

In live market trading it helps to keep the decision making process as consistent and objective as possible. Using a rules based plan for your trading is a *must* and is a trait all successful investors and traders I know possess. A winning plan should be able to sustain your profitability over time in order that you can *keep* all your hard earned profits you make from the markets. Your simple rule based strategy should *only* have you buying at price levels where demand (wholesale prices) exceeds supply and selling at price levels where supply (retail prices) exceeds demand.

The reality of it is that too many undisciplined new traders don't spend enough time composing a rules based plan for the type of trading they wish to do. I have my clients think about what their monetary goals are and then help them compose a great trading plan, becoming a great trader, and attaining their goals.

There is *no room for excuses* in the professional traders mind and thus they know that they are the final decision maker on what is being done or *NOT* done.

They are in complete control of all aspects of their trading plan. They have mastered keeping their emotions fully controlled and are aware they are in control of the destiny of there long term investment strategy and management of their portfolio. This is one of the things that make them so successful and it is *all done by following their rule based plan*.

Let me paint a couple of different pictures for you *right up front* so you can get a picture of what it will be like going in the live markets *without* a rule based plan and unprepared or even underprepared in *your* mind. This will give you an idea of what can happen by not having or using a rule based plan in your trading and investing business.

Think of yourself on a nice vacation down in beautiful Australia and you are out sport fishing somewhere around the Great Barrier Reef.

Now you are preparing to set your line but need to get your chum (bait) out first and as you are working on the chum you accidently cut a very deep gash into your leg around your Femoral artery, *and* just at *the* moment you do *that* a rogue wave hits the boat and knocks you *and* the chum bucket overboard and into the water. Now you are the water bleeding profusely *with the chum* and the 21 foot great white sharks that frequent the area you are fishing in. It is said that great white sharks can smell blood in the water for 1000 nautical miles and be in the area in a nanosecond. You can finish this one however *you* like but the sharks win.

The second one is real easy. Imagine you have some huge cajones and you decide you are going play Russian roulette with a loaded revolver that's *fully* loaded. As the song says "click click BOOM"! Only *you* are the one who is going to get FUBAR. That's what you'll be doing by going in the live market unprepared and without a plan. You can kid yourself all you want and say "it will never happen to me" however trust me *it will*.

While these examples may seem harsh to you if you are brand new and have zero experience and are looking for information to get you started in the trading and investing business just remember them when you are screwing around on demo doing all the kooky stuff you *will* do. Demo is where you can do all that crazy stuff you will try, like trading 20 cars on crude oil or gold with no plan. Get it *alllll* out of your system in demo though because the sharks are waiting for you in the live market. The sharks just *might* hand you a loaded revolver so be prepared.

I tell *all* new people I help out that what you will find is that over the course of your learning curve and time in the live markets that you will ultimately find that what is going to work for you and make you money every day or month is a combination of things you have learned over time and have put together to make *your own* winning rule based plan. What works for one trader *will not* work the same way for another however that does not mean you cannot adapt different ideas to fit your own trading style.

Developing a trading plan takes a lot of hard work sometimes as much if not more than actually learning how to trade and operate your platform. It takes time to see what works for you and what does not. It also takes a lot of time to develop the rules that go along with your trading plan. Having a plan and some rules are critical in this business. To not have them and stick to them is a recipe for financial disaster and account ruin.

It doesn't matter how many or how few rules you have in your plan. Most investors and traders I know who are consistently profitable on a daily basis have a simple plan that is perhaps one page or less. It is one thing to have a plan it is however the most important thing to do is to *follow the plan at all costs*. I always say if you are a known rule breaker then just don't too many however you must have *some*.

One exercise I like my clients to do to get them in the habit of following their plan is to pretend they are an airline pilot and they have to follow a checklist at all times and never break any procedural rules or all lives could be lost. Airline pilots by the way are some of the best investors and traders out there in the business today. They are used to doing what I just described and will not deviate for any reason.

Take the last paragraph and just imagine that your account balance is the lives and if you do not follow your plan *all* of your money could be lost. Make no mistake you can perhaps lose *all* of your money by not having and following a plan.

Successful investors and traders know that that having a simple plan is the only way to have a profitable significant *edge* in the live markets. A plan does not have to be complicated to be successful and these consistently profitable investors and traders have come to realize this and actually use the simplest methods in investing and trading which as I said, is supply and demand.

One of the things that traders do is they get monitoring their positions confused with trade management. If you have followed your rules based plan and determined your entry and exit as well as your stop loss and profit target there should be nothing to do really.

What I mean by monitoring your position is to make sure your automated strategy if you are using one is doing what it is supposed to be doing. This is critical as even the best automated strategy can have a discombobulation at some point.

I only recommend using an automated system if you are using it for putting on and taking off positions as well as executing a stop loss and profit target at the same time as the position is being executed in the live market. Then it is truly hands off. All you need to do at that point is to **keep your hands off** the mouse and let the market do all the heavy lifting for you. *Can* you do that?

Until you can monitor your live market positions without actually doing *anything* I strongly recommend that you *stay out* of the real live market with your hard earned real money. Just because you are monitoring what is going on *does not* mean you have to take any action!

The sooner you can get your head around that last statement *the more money* you will be able to make. That's is what you are in this business for so have some control and do what needs to be done to become successful. Be disciplined and don't make the mistakes this book details. Do not become one of the sheeple of the herd and do what everyone else does and study what everyone else studies.

Your job now as a professional investor and trader is to manage your money and control risk at *all* costs. You are basing all of the decisions you make on your developed logic not with emotions. You are confident that you would much rather pursue a low risk entry or have only a small loss if it should happen. It is only low risk, high reward and high probability outcomes that you are looking for now, just like the Wall Street banks and the smart money.

I recommend that if you are not able to give investing and trading your full-time attention, you should have your money managed by someone qualified *who does it for a living*. Learn as much as you can about the trading business, and then when you are ready, you can make the transition to doing it as a full-time business for yourself. You can certainly do the learning and education phase of this business part time however you *absolutely should not do* the trading part of it part time.

Learn to think independently and make *unlimited* money for yourself for the rest of your life!

Its world class competition and you need to have an edge to make high profits

You must know what you want to get out of trading the financial markets *before* you do anything or study anything. What is the reason you are considering doing this business? You must be prepared to go into the live markets with the best market participants in the world. What? You thought you were going to be in there alone?

The market is a game. The competition is of universal proportions. The novice retail investor or trader has an enormous handicap. They often aren't even aware they are playing a game; let alone what the rules are. The smart money are the makers of the market, hence the deciders of the rules in the *live* market, and it is as I said, competition at the **absolute highest level**. Why, because it involves money. You had better be *well-prepared* and *well-funded* to compete with the top traders in the world. If you think that you are going to get your one lot filled at a supply and demand value area before the smart money *I have news for you.*

You are not only competing with the smart money at supply and demand value areas on the chart for entry. You are also competing against *all the other professional traders in the entire world* who "*get it.*" The live market is competition at the universal level as I have said, and it is *imperative* that you be well armed to battle against the best people in the world.

The smart money moves the market with all their money. However, it is all the other people who you are competing with for entry that you have to be prepared for. One way you can increase your chances of beating them is to place your order in the market before they do. By 'front running' as it is called, the smart money and the other competition, you can gain entry before them and get paid by everyone who enters after you. This includes the smart money if you should, by some chance, beat them to a fill. There is also actually another *very easy way* to beat them to a fill before they take PA to the value area. You can just click the mouse and buy/sell at market and *make* them fill you.

How do you *make them* fill you may be asking? The answer is very simple and I already said it above. All YOU have to do is press the button and you're in, *BOOM*. Then what? You better have your SL pre planned and your exit if you trade in that manner all mapped out. Live action is not going to wait for you to figure it out. I have a NT ATM strategy that enters all orders at the click of the mouse upon entry. No fumbling around at all.

You are now asking what about slippage? I liken slippage to paying the cover at the strip club, you want to see titties right? You pay the $20 cover or whatever it is, *BOOM* you see the titties. In the live market if you want to make money with the big boys and use a market order to do so, you pay the cover, slippage.

Remember they are the Wall Street banks and all the rest of the biggest players in the world you are messing with in that area. They can stay at a price level *waaaaaay* longer than your account can remain solvent *so remember that.* For me, it's about seeing *where* they are, and trading *with* them not against them, *try it and you will surely get* FUBAR!!

Once a retail trader can understand the markets and what makes them work, *that* being supply and demand, he or she can begin to identify where and when the smart money is going to turn the market. With this realization, the retail trader has a decent chance to compete in the game.

The smart money doesn't want you to know about this type supply and demand trading so it is commonly not taught. I know of only maybe two educators who teach this method of investing and trading and I am fairly certain they have to travel with body guards—I am kidding but you get the point. If you want to get your, investing and trading business on track to make money every day in the live markets, I strongly encourage you to learn how to spot what the smart money is doing in the live market, and then *follow their lead.*

Here is something else for you to always remember, you are not in the market alone. The market is full of educated people who know more than you'll *ever* know and have bigger capital than **you'll** ***ever*** **have**. You are competing with Wall Street banks, hedge funds, mutual funds etc. Educate yourself to be a competitor and a winner. You want to have success, right? You need to be prepared to work with the best in the world because that's who's in there.

The other thing you always need to remember is that you are *also* competing against the machines, not just the best human investors and traders. You still have to compete with the HFT's, Algo, and AMM's and they work in nanoseconds. Do you? *You don't* unless you trade from a super computer like they do.

The professionals are *only interested in making money* and doing it by taking a longer term view. The smart money does not day trade. They have billion dollar super computers and code slinging geeks making a cool million a year for doing nothing but writing computer algorithms to tell the computer what to do, what to see and what trades to take. These people are in the business of making money with money, which most of the time is *yours*.

You need to be on point need and at the top of your game when pulling the trigger with your assets. Your rules should be set in concrete by now, and you should be able to see the smart money value areas at a glance, without even drawing lines on them. When you make the decision to go live with real money, that's when it gets serious for you. You are now in competition with the big boys who have billions of dollars to play with and have the best technology in the world.

You absolutely need to have a competitive edge in the markets, and you must have it *before* you do anything in the live markets with real money. If you run with the 'sheeple of the herd' you can be assured to not have any edge. They all study the same information and are all programmed the same way to lose money repeatedly.

A competitive edge includes a mental edge with discipline, laser focus, and a fail-proof strategy. Enforcing some rules in your strategy is critical and following them at all costs will absolutely make sure you can beat the competition. I always say that if you are a known rule breaker, then just don't establish too many. However, the ones you *do* have must be followed *as if your very life depended on them*. Your account balance certainly does!

In the live market there are people who are looking to take *all* your money and are willing to walk over dead bodies to get paid and rest assured they will walk right into your account and drain it like it's your life blood. They don't know you; care if you are having a bad day at the office or lose all your money to them in the live market because it is just business as usual to them on an everyday basis. The smart money is the Wall Street Banks, institutions, hedge funds, HFT's and dark pools.

They are the liquidity providers and market makers. They, as well as the sheeple of the herd are whom you need to be able to see on a price chart if you want to make money in the financial markets.

When you think you are going to try to *shortcut it* just remember there are sharks with fully loaded revolvers in the live market *waiting for you* to take that shortcut so they can take all your money. You can also just think of the smoke and flames coming out of your barbeque because you threw all your money in there, and didn't have a rule based plan as to how to work in the live markets where you are in competition with sharks. There are *no shortcuts* to your success in investing and trading. You have to do the time if you want to drive the money train.

You must develop and have a Wall Street mindset to gain high profits every day

Banks and institutions are in the business to make money plain and simple. All they care about are two things and that is *time* and *price* which I have talked a bit about already in the book. The only thing they are in business for is to make a profit. Who are they making the all the loot from though? It's *you* the retail trader that's who. They can see they retail sheeple of the herd making their mistakes on a price chart and just take advantage of them over and over and over again on a daily basis.

It's no secret that Wall Street banks make huge profits. It is in your face in the media on a daily basis. How do they actually make this huge profit though? They make their huge profits by controlling their risk on the *every* position they take. *All they care about* is protecting their risk capital when it is exposed in the live markets. We are talking about in the billions of dollars perhaps even a trillion dollars at any given moment.

Professional traders don't think like Main Street they think like Wall Street. If you want to become very successful in this business you must develop a Wall Street mentality when it comes to making money. There is just *no* other option. If you study what the Wall Street banks and the hedge fund people are doing and then emulate their performance you can make a nice living in the markets.

Every professional investor and trader I associate with treats investing and trading as a business *and so should you*. Having a plan to do your business is the most important aspect of making money in the investing and trading business especially when your real money is on the line in the live market. If you wish to be a consistently profitable investor and trader in today's live market and survive, build your plan to do so. Build your plan around what you're intended goals are the Wall Street banks do.

Trading to win every day is what these professional people and the Wall Street banks do. You are looking at the same information on your charts as every other trader in the world looking at that chart you are on. The question is do *you* see it how *they* see it? You need to see what the banks and institutions see and you also need to be able to spot the sheeple of the herd retail traders making their mistakes also. *You can profit from both groups if you know how and are prepared properly to do so.*

When you have learned how to read the price action of the instruments you have chosen to work in to make you money in the live market you should have no problems making money with the smart money. The markets are there for everyone to make money every day all you have to do is go in there and get it. I always say "see what they see do what they do".

The only problem with that is that *everyone else* is trying to do that also. It all goes back to preparedness to work in the live market. If you should decide to go in there and are unprepared or even underprepared you will assuredly lose some money right away and perhaps even *all* of it. Don't be *that* trader!

It will take you a long time to get to this point however hopefully you will. You *will* realize that you don't need to be in the market all the time to actually make a lot of money. The more you use the right tools of the trade as it were the more you will see that the real money making professionals are only deploying their capital in the live market when there is a reason to do so.

They follow their rule based plan which tells them all the parameters of when they actually need to be in the market. There is a big difference between wanting to be in the market and *needing* to be in the market. This all goes back to studying the right information from the beginning. If you are a brand new trader I strongly encourage you to just take your time and read this book through again slower the next time.

There is a reason there are no charts in this book. I would like it if you could actually absorb what has been written here because if you can just sit back and think it all through logically I am sure you will realize that you can become *very successful* in this business if you can have some patience and develop and rule based plan that is based on the type of investing and trading you wish to do.

Here is one thing for you to think about when deciding on what type of investor or trader you desire to be. The more action you desire the more money you are going to pay for that action in the form of fees and commissions to your broker. Just remember the more money you throw away on that kind of thing *the less money you will have* to grow your wealth over the long term and make money with money.

Most professional traders including myself swing trade and position trade. If you want to do what the smart money does *this is it*. They don't look at intraday charts. They are in the business of making money with money. That is only done on daily and long term charts, with a long term perspective in mind.

Many people say that money doesn't buy happiness and while that *is* true, a lot of it *can* buy a Gulfstream 650! I hate standing in line at the airport don't you? Do what it says in this book and you could be on your way owning your own G650.

As I have said before you have to be willing to have a "kill everyone" mentality to work in the live markets. Professional traders know that there are people in the live markets who will walk over dead bodies to get paid and have no qualms about following the smart money to where they are going. Professionals let the smart money lead the way and do all of the dirty work, moving and shaking with their money and volume. *Why not just learn to do the same?* You must develop a *cold* and *ruthless* as well as decisive personality to work in the live market with the people who are looking to kill your account.

Should you decide to try going up against these type traders in the live market and be under funded or under prepared or *not prepared at all* as I said, they will carve up your account like it is a Thanksgiving turkey you *can be assured of that.*

The smart money is not your worst enemy in the market, although they are not trying to be your best friend either. They *do* however leave clues in the market that are up you to decipher and then act upon without hesitation or fear. Are they doing this to be nice to you? *I doubt it!* They just cannot hide some of the clues they leave. Once you know what you are looking for, you can take advantage of the clues and make a low risk, high reward entry into the market and have a high probability outcome.

Unfortunately, most retail investors and traders do not take advantage of these signals that the smart money leaves behind. They do a lot of damage to their accounts because of it. They actually try to do the opposite of what the smart money does, and end up on the wrong end of the market every time, thus causing themselves to lose money.

The smart money follows the path of least resistance to supply and demand areas. They show you the way. All you need to do is mimic their moves and you can make some money every day in the live markets. They can do all the heavy lifting, *so why not just let them*?

The harsh reality of the market is that there are people in there who are trying to take your money and transfer it from your account to theirs. Are you going to *let* that happen? By now if you have read this far, this book has *totally* scared the crap out of you. That is probably a good thing and you should take note. If you are brand new and want to really *do* this business and are not just playing around you should plan to *not* do these mistakes and take as long as you need to take with your learning curve. The market is *always* going to be there waiting to pay you!

It is very easy for them to see the retail trader on the price chart because they are always making the same mistakes over and over and over again. *They do it all day every day.* Who do you think pays the smart money? Where do you think the smart money gains their profits from? I will tell you. It's *you*.

They *know* you are trading a scared money account and will make the same mistakes again and again. They *know* that you are your own worst enemy in the market not them. Do yourself a *huge* favor and **get the right education and training from day one** and you will have a chance at working with the best traders in the world and make an *unlimited* amount of money until you reach *your number*. What is it?

How it will all come together

If you are willing to put in the time and do some the things that this book suggests, you can certainly be on your way to driving your money train down the golden tracks to the front door of your bank every day. There are a number of steps you *must* go through to get to a level of understanding of the financial markets and how they actually work to be able to make money on a consistent daily basis *and be able to keep it.*

Once you have the method of using supply and demand down pat and can see what you need to see on a live price chart you should have zero problems pulling the trigger on a trade buy just pushing the buy/sell button or having your order resting in the market waiting for PA to come and give you what you want.

You will be able to see your competition making their mistakes over and over again. You can then take advantage of them just like *we* all do and get paid from them every day. Remember for every buyer there *has* to be a seller and for every seller there *has* to be a buyer, which means *someone has to win,* and *someone has to lose.* Which do you plan on being? Are you going to be the one paying the competition or are going to be the one *getting paid*?

My final advice to newbie beginner Forex traders

Listen don't fuck around, investing and trading or the business of making money with money as I like to call it, is dead serious and should you try to get cute, fancy or try to sidestep *any part* of the learning for doing it only one thing will happen, you'll get **FUBAR and lose all of your money**. Matter of fact, all of the professionals are counting on you doing so (getting fancy) in order for them to continue to profit from you, and continue transferring your account to theirs, *is that what you want?*

I'm just trying to give you the brutal truth in trading, and if you're not ready to handle it then you should wait to begin this business until you are, can you Jack screaming *"YOU CAN'T HANDLE THE TRUTH"*. I get a lot of flak from others for letting beginners know what's up however I know it is falling on deaf ears most of the time so I don't really worry about it too much.

I also get a lot of flak for talking about S&D trading and giving some details of how it works in the live markets. People always say why are you giving it away, I'm not really giving any secrets away honestly. *The markets only work on supply and demand and always will,* it's nothing fancy which is why most new traders get in trouble, they think it is complex and it's not.

The reality of the live markets is that there are people in there who are smarter than you, have *waaaaaaaay* more money than you, have better algo than you and are trying to take your money and transfer it from your account to theirs. They don't know you, care about you, or have any feelings if you are having a bad day at the office and lose all your damn money. It's just business. The business of making money with money and it is always *your* money. Don't be *that* trader. Learn to do this business the right way from the beginning and you won't be.

Trading in today's financial markets it is competition at the very top level, where the stakes are the highest. Educate yourself to be a competitor and a winner. You want to have success, right? You need to be prepared to work with the best market participants in the world. That's who are in there in the live financial markets and *they are looking to kill your account*. Don't get killed!

The best advice I can give you is *not to enter* the live market with real money until you are ready. It's really that simple. No one is making you do this business. You are the boss and in control of what you are doing, *so have some*. Entering the live market and using real money before you are fully ready and confident enough to do so will only cause you to lose money and question your skills.

If you just think about what this book is telling you to do logically, *and* what to study, you can soon be driving you're new Ferrari down the road paved of gold right to the front door of your bank to deposit all of your profits from the success from your new Forex investing and trading business.

All the different types of investors and traders I know use a rule based plan. They all have different rules for the different methods they trade. Their strict adherence to their rule based plan ensures that they have the edge needed to go into the live markets every day with zero fear and have the confidence in knowing that by following the plan they will be giving themselves the best possible opportunity for a high probability positive outcome and ensuring their long term survival in the live markets.

To really succeed at trading the financial markets, you need to not only _thoroughly_ understand risk reward, position sizing, and risk amount per trade, you also need to consistently execute each of these aspects of money management in combination with a highly effective yet simple to understand trading strategy like price action and supply and demand principles.

Having a plan and sticking to it is one thing that all investors and traders must overcome to be a successful market participant for a long term financial benefit. This should be the goal of anyone considering a business or career in the investing and trading business. Making _some_ money every day should be the goal of all investors and traders no matter what asset class you are working in. This is easier said than done though.

Brand new traders tend to self-sabotage their own efforts at the beginning of their trading careers and businesses because they had not learned that there is a lot to know and have mastered before one can become successful in this business. There are a lot of different things we can do to improve our trading, but there are also things we can do to sabotage our trading as well. One of those things is not *getting* or *having* enough information.

It is my goal in this book to give you the information that can help you right from the start of your new trading business *the first day*. It is so important for traders to start out right from the beginning because the outcome of not having done so is *very expensive* and no one likes to or wants to lose money. Unfortunately brand new investors and traders tend to lose almost all of their money on their first try in the markets.

The average brand new investor or trader who does not do the proper education and training right from the start loses twenty one thousand dollars on average in the first three months of live trading and an average of forty five thousand dollars in their first year. That's ugly if you ask me. *I'll take the forty large if you're just going to throw it out.*

Almost all brand new investors and traders make the mistakes in this book when they first start out. Now that you have read this entire book and know what *not to do* you can have a head start to driving your money train to the bank on a daily basis. I encourage you to read to other books in my beginner's series as they detail how to become consistently profitable right from the start of your business.

You absolutely need to have a competitive edge in the markets, and you *must* have it *before* you do anything in the live markets with real money. I know I probably sound like a broken record in saying that by now however if you don't develop your edge *before* going into the live financial markets *you're the one who will be broke(n)*. If you run with the 'sheeple of the herd' you can be assured to *not* have any edge. They all study the same information and are all programmed the same way to lose money repeatedly. Don't be *that* trader! Always follow the smart money!

Make no mistake this is a dead serious business and *you should treat that way*. You as a retail investor or trader have a limited chance of having a positive outcome in the live market against the best market participants in the world, not to mention having to try to make money from the machines. It is said that 70% of the market making is done by super computers now. You *can't* beat them however you *can* train yourself to see what they are doing on a price chart and then make money *with* them.

I like to think of it (the market) as a big bank ATM machine because it is open virtually 24 hours a day seven days a week just about. You just need to have the proper PIN# to get your money out. Do the training and education and *do not* make these mistakes in this book and you will be well on your way to having your own personal PIN# to make *unlimited* money in the live markets every day. While the market *is* like a big ATM that is open 24 hours a day if you **don't** have the *right* PIN# *your money will get sucked into it,* of that you can be assured.

As I said to make it in this business you must have the 3 p's patience, persistence and perseverance. Here are some extra **tips** I can give you. If I have said it once I have said it 100 million times. Trade smart **OR JUST DON'T TRADE**! If you have to use leverage you should not be investing or trading with real money. Only invest or trade with money that is disposable and can't hurt you if you lose *all* of it. Learn this business right from the beginning on day one. Don't become one of the sheeple of the herd and study what everyone else is doing.

When the market you are working is volatile *take smaller positions.* **Always feel free to take your profit; the market is always going to be there with more.** *Only* be in the market when the liquidity providers are there providing liquidity. You should only *be in* the market if your rule based plan has told you to be in the market and all of the criteria of your plan for executing a live position are there.

Do what the smart money does *where* they do it at and you have a much higher probability of a positive outcome! Trade what you see happening *NOT* what you *THINK* is *GOING* to happen, you can only do this by using supply and demand to trade with. You can't lose any money in the market if you're *not in it*. Never *ever* enter a trend after it has begun, you will only be diminishing your profit margin and increasing your risk. **Never** enter a position when the PA is sideways, hence the *CHOP SHOP*.

If you don't really see an S&D level then hey guess what, ***don't enter***!! You don't have to always *be in* the market. If you just *wait* till PA gets to where you need it to be for you to get what you want *you'll get what you want*. Let the market do all the heavy lifting for you. Only do what you know to be true when working in the live market. The value areas are quite easy to spot once you have trained your eye to look at current price action and then look up and left. Spot them, draw your lines accordingly, then *wait (I said wait goddamit!)* for PA to come back and fill your resting order you have waiting. If you are using an automated strategy which I *strongly* encourage you to do, all you will have to do is sit back and wait to get paid. The best advice I can give you is, **always use a stop** and ___keep your hand off___ that damn mouse!!

Finally it is all about being organized and disciplined. Successful traders have this down pat. They have developed their trading edge over time and have mastered it and built their trading plan around this edge. Some of these traders even go as far as writing their plan out on paper and keeping it with them at all times. It takes a lot of time and patience to develop this type of system and these investors and traders have taken the appropriate amount of time to get it down which in turn has made them into consistently profitable and successful market participants. *Isn't that what you want to be*?

One *last* thing I can leave you with. Remember the smoke and flames coming out of your barbeque because you threw all your money in there and didn't have a rule based plan as to how to work in the live markets, where you are in competition with sharks that are waiting to hand you a loaded revolver that is fully loaded.

Here is one more visual I can give you to solidify how important it is being prepared and competing in the market with an edge over your competition. Remember in the movie Jaws when the boat captain got devoured whole by the shark? He was a stupid ass and went after an advisory underprepared hence the line "you're gonna need a bigger boat". Just imagine your *whole capital account* is Quint the boat captain going down the throat of the shark whole, that's what will happen in the live market should you decide to go in there without an edge and a proper education, except you'll be saying "I'm gonna need more capital".

Like I said, it's a friggin brutal business so let this be your wakeup call!

Bonus section

I put this bonus section in my new trader books because I feel it can help you get a huge head start in developing your edge for working in the live markets. It took me years to find this information and now I give to you in this book as a bonus. *You're welcome!*

This bonus section is just a glimpse of what it is going to take to become successful in the live markets. If you are brand new to this business here are some ideas for using your time in the best way. You first obviously need to have a grasp on all of the data in the above sections. There is a lot of work to do and I hope this section can give you some ideas as to what you need to do.

Demo trading or simulated trading to get the practice of putting on a position and taking off a position is good. It is good for learning how to place your SL and PT and manage them if you work that way. Demo trading is very good to get to know how your software platform works and how to use all the tools it offers you. Drawing lines on your value areas, mapping PA etc.

If you don't have a lot of time right when you first get into this business to practice trading on demo during regular market sessions then what you can do is record the session and then trade it at a time when you can practice. I recommend that you get a trading platform that enables you to do this as it will help you to *cut down* your learning curve and practice time greatly. You want to be in there making *REAL* money don't you? *Do what needs to be done and get it done*!!!

I would like you to always remember that simulated/demo trading *is just that*. You are **not** trading against anyone so it does not really matter what you are doing. There is no one on other side of what you're doing. It is great for learning your chosen platform and learning your system/method. You do have a method or system and a rule based plan *right*? Remember on demo it's really about practicing your strategy and entries and exit's and *that's it*. It will not work the same in the live market so you should prepare yourself with that in mind.

http://www.informedtrades.com/index.php has a huge amount of *free* courses for the brand new investor and trader. Simit the owner over there has done a fine job at compiling all the data and information that a brand new investor and trader will need to know and can study there *for free*. You can journal there and also perhaps get your questions answered by other investors and traders to help you expedite your learning curve.

I encourage you to study and use supply and demand trading. You can find a great *free* supply and demand learning thread here: http://www.forexfactory.com/showthread.php?t=4282 04 Alfonso over there does an awesome job and goes above and beyond what any trader should do to teach new traders supply and demand trading. You should buy him a Ferrari when you become successful. Don't worry that it is a Forex related thread; supply and demand trading works on *any* liquid asset class on *any* time frame you chose to look at and trade from.

Go there and learn with the other new traders who are there. All the rules of using supply and demand for trading are listed on the first page of the thread. There are *plenty* of chart examples as well. You can also do a search online for a foundation and application course for supply and demand. They are online ***for free*** for anyone who can find the information. There are only 2-3 people who teach this type of trading and you should learn it from whomever you understand the best and are the most comfortable with.

All successful investors and traders I know have a daily pre-market routine. They all do the same thing to prepare for the market every day, the same way, all the time. They are in the habit of doing this every single day. They have a checklist of what their routine is and go down the list every day. They have their notes from their analysis right there so they can see them at a glance.

One of the reasons why professional traders have become successful is because they know what they are going to do *before* they take any action. It is one of the traits that all professionals I know have. They would not *even think* of going into the live market with their real money without having quantified what the price action of the asset they are working in is doing.

You can get a free demo account on think or swim by just calling. Normally the feed is delayed by 15 minutes. I believe however if you call and ask the technical services person who answers the call you can get them to make it so your feed is in real time. This is important in the sense that if you need to make a real time decision to acquire a position the 15 minute delay could be a problem for that.

Here are a couple of capital scenarios for a beginning day trader or swing trader. You can begin to trade immediately in the live market with real on money *on as little as $500*. Once you have completed your training and education, become consistently profitable on demo and composed your rule based plan for the type of investing and trading you wish to do you can then begin to trade in the live markets with real money.

The live market environment is the only place you can make real money with your account so you should *do it as soon as possible*. By trading live right away you will also be able to test your rule based plan and the criteria you have developed to execute live market positions. If it is not going to work in the live market the market will let you know *right away* trust me on that. The only way you can make real money is to use real money! By trading live right away you will be able to experience both the *good* and *bad* feelings of investing and trading live with real money. You'll find that you become much more emotional when trading real money.

The **only way** to trade in real time as a beginner in the live market with real money and do it **on a $500 account size** is to trade micro Forex or micro-cap stocks. Only these two types of instruments would allow you to get a taste of the live market with real money and see if everything you have done up to this point *will actually work in real time live with real money*. I recommend that all brand new investors and traders start out in this way due to the brutality and volatility of the markets. Brand new investors and traders have no idea what it will be like in the live market using their real money until they actually do it.

Once you become proficient and consistently profitable with smaller lot or share sizes, you can then just scale you're trading. Once you experience consistent profitable success with small positions, instead of trading more instruments just increase the number of lot or shares for each position.

Model yourself repeatedly after highly successful traders – adopting both their attitudes and behaviors. Find a successful trader or investor or one of each and study them. Look at hedge fund owners who have returned 20% or more over a prolonged period of time. Study them then try to develop a style which emulates this successful method and make one of your own. Before you know it *YOU* will be the one making 20% or more in your business.

The absolute biggest advantage when it comes to being successful in investing and trading, is having stuck with it. That's when you can feel good and know that no one did it but you. The more you try to find the Holy Grail and jump from method to method the less chance you will have to succeed in investing and trading, hence the 97% failure rate. Those of us who *HAVE* made it and *ARE* successful have traveled a *looooong* road, *which we now cruise our Ferraris on*. JK

One of the most common traits all of the successful investors and traders I know is that they all use a journal. If you get into the practice of writing down all of your trades in a journal the information in there can be invaluable to you should you hit a rough patch of trading. Trust me **everyone** hits a rough patch at some point.

To become consistently profitable and successful in investing and trading can be a long and very expensive learning curve. To go from being a novice who makes a lot of mistakes to a professional who avoids making them like their life depended on it takes quite a bit of time. A journal can help cut down the time it takes and also help with the learning process everyone must go through.

You might think it takes too much time to journal all your trades however the time you take while doing it is what can be the greatest value of all. The more data you write down the better idea you can have of what is working and what did not work. The journal can and should be used as a self-education tool to further your trading career. I know of no successful professional investor or trader who has not used a journal. They only act on a position if the data points to having had a low risk high reward high probability outcome.

One of the first questions I ask anyone who comes to me for mentoring help is if they use a journal in their trading and if so how long they have been doing it. The information I can look at in the journal can help me to ascertain how I can help them right from the start. I can see their strengths, weaknesses and if they are biased toward any type of trading. I can also look at how they can improve their efficiency and make suggestions on other data they may add to their journal.

In addition to the technical aspects of your trading you record in the journal you can also include how the market was acting, the sentiment, and what the conditions were that caused you to enter a position. Recording this type of data in your journal will give you a reference point to see what conditions you set that were met that gave you the highest probability for having a positive outcome in the market at that time.

Most investors and traders like to think they are very decisive and disciplined. Then they go back and read the notes in their journal and find out they made some mistakes and perhaps even may have deviated from their trading plan. This information can be a good thing in the sense that it will help to improve any problems which may be arising in the daily work in the market.

You must be able rationalize why you did things the way you did them when in the live market. You are in control of all the variables that enable you to have a positive outcome as a market participant. So have some control and journal why you did it a certain way. No one is making you do this business but you.

I always tell clients to think like they are a money manager of a hedge fund or mutual fund. I have them think about how they would explain their choice on entering a position to their client and what the client would think of their reasons to having their money entered into the live market in this manner. If you can't convince the client how do you convince yourself?

Once you have your desired template and the data which you would like to have in the journal you can go back and see your winning positions and then work to emulate those conditions in the future in the live market over and over again. Seeing what you did where and when you did it for a positive outcome can give you trading an edge that will last you forever.

Having a winning edge is what separates the consistently profitable investors and traders from the sheeple of the herd. When you can see what you did right and know what they are doing wrong you can capitalize on their mistakes and realize more profits.

Over time as your account balance builds up it will be just be a matter of adding more size to your positions when entering the same way you have been doing it all along on the winners. That's how *serious money* is made in the markets. If you have learned how to see where the supply and demand value areas are on the price chart this will only add to your edge and give you the confidence to enter with the smart money with zero fear.

Over the long run you will just develop the habits of taking a position without even thinking about it when your conditions are met in the market. The reason is because you have reviewed what works over and over again in the analysis you have done on your journal and know what works when and also more importantly what does not.

Another way that the journal can be of great assistance is in your morning routine. You do have a morning routine *don't you*? You can use the journal as a way to see what times in the market you have been working in that the liquidity providers are providing liquidity as that is the only time you should be in the market anyway.

You can tell where the supply and demand value areas are going to be because you have already mapped them out and recorded the data in the journal for future reference. It is these value areas that you want to be trading from and taking your profits at. You can even assign them a points system so that you can know when the best time to enter will be.

I suggest you develop a morning routine. Get into the habit of doing the same thing every day all the time. Here is a good morning routine to start getting in the habit of doing every day before you go in the live market to work. Turn on your charts. While the charts are booting up review your journal and any notes you have made. OK charts are up. Look at current PA where is it in relation to the London and Asian sessions? Where is it in relation to the previous day's session? Now look above and left and below and left and see where current PA is. Where are the value areas? Where is the curve at? Draw your S&D value area lines accordingly, and then trade according to your plan.

As a brand new trader and investor you should fully realize that no one book is going to give you all of the information that you need to have to be able to make a living at trading. While there are entire books written on the subjects this book covers. This book is written to tell beginning Forex day traders and investors how to do just that, begin.

Everyone has to start somewhere in this business and you must have the right information from the very first day if you want to become successful in this business. You don't need to know everything all at one time nor could you. You don't have to learn how to trade every asset class and how to become an expert in every conceivable aspect of trading. You should concentrate on becoming a *specialist* versus being a *generalist*.

You should focus on one market at a time and *become an expert at it*. This will enable you to make a very good living. A trader friend of mine said to me one time. "Why do you want to learn a bunch of markets when you can just add another contract to what you are already doing that is making you money"? It was like he punched me in the face. Talk about an AHHHA moment!!

Supply and demand trading is by no means the only way to trade the markets, *it is* however the *only* thing that makes price move in a market and you need to fully understand that and have a complete grasp of the principles of supply and demand to be a money maker and have an edge in the live markets.

All brand new traders think they need some magic indicator or system to make money in the markets and that could not be further from the truth. This book has given you the **truth in trading** which is that the markets only work on supply and demand, *period*! Honestly, the sooner you can wrap your head around what I just said the more money you make in the live markets.

You can do anything you want on a demo platform because no one is on the other side of your trade. When you try to do all that crazy stuff you do on demo in the real world in the real markets you will undoubtedly lose *some* or perhaps even *all* of your hard earned money so don't you owe it to yourself to learn this business the right way from the first day with the best information?

If you go into the market without having done the work required to learn this business thoroughly the market <u>will</u> punish you beyond your wildest imagination *make no mistake of that*. You might think you can learn a couple of chart patterns and set ups and perhaps a little risk management but trust me when I say that all of us who are in the market every day and make money in the market everyday can see you coming a mile away and know that you have not fully prepared and educated yourself.

Your lack of education and knowledge makes you stand out like a sore thumb in the live market and you can be seen making the same mistakes over and over and over again in the same way all the time and those professionals and smart money players just capitalize on the lack of education and knowledge that the brand new investor and trader has until they do finally *"get it"* or we have taken all of their money and transferred it from their account to ours. That's *all* the market is really is a transfer of accounts and money to those who know what they are doing and are completely prepared, and work from a rules based plan at all times from those who do not.

The best thing about the market is that it is there every day waiting to pay out the trader who is ready to do business. There are brand new people stepping into the live market every day who are in no way, shape or form ready to deal with the brutality or volatility that can happen in a nanosecond in the live markets on a daily basis. Those of us who work in there and know *what to do* and *when to do it* just capitalize and make our money from those who don't know what the hell just hit them. *Which trader do you want to be?*

Listen don't take my word for it, talk to some real money traders and investors and ask them questions. I was fortunate to be brought into the business by someone who was a real money trader and then found a mentor later on after I was already trading with my own real money. He was able to help me move to the professional level.

My choosing to write this book for all the brand new traders and investors just in the beginning stages of their learning curve is the reason I feel there is nothing out there that tells you everything that is important to know to make real money versus just telling you something that will help you learn to trade. The business of making money with money is *very serious* and you should have your head on straight *before* you ever begin to use real money to work with.

I have no "system" or magic indicators that will go "ding" and tell you when to enter a trade to try to sell you. No hopium pills here. Just the *real world* information that you need that will help you to become a consistently profitable trader with an edge on a daily basis if you follow what it says to do in here in this book. I don't have a fancy "trading room" or service to try to sell you, hell I don't even have a freakin website.

I am fortunate that I *actually do live* the trader lifestyle everyone is so keen on attaining. I have chosen a way of trading that allows me to have all of the free time I could ever want or need and still make plenty of money. That is why I am able to sit down and write a book like this for all of the brand new people who want to get into this business and need some basic starting information from someone who actually *really is* a swing trader and investor and not someone who is just a book marketer.

I *strongly* recommend that any new trader tries to find a mentor if possible; a professional real money investor or trader who can answer questions from a real, live market perspective, someone who only invests and trades with real money. Experienced investors and traders can be of great value to the novice retail trader due to their knowledge base and their developed mental abilities to work in the markets full-time, using real money.

New investors and traders have a lack of psychological knowledge that in the beginning is a detriment to them, and they are their own worst enemy at this point. I would call or text my mentor and say I just did *this* or *that*, and he would just say, "In real money?"

I had doubled my demo account four months in a row on demo. Then instead of resetting it again, I let it go and took it up to over three hundred thousand dollars. Once I had done this, he urged me to go in the live market and see if I could really do it with real money. I finally went live and never looked back. I still have an occasional losing day now and then, though. No one is perfect. *No one*!

What I mean by a losing day is not making *any* money and *giving the market* some of my own money. That is my definition of a losing day. What's yours? I would rather light myself on fire or eat broken glass and wash it down with gasoline than give the market any of my own capital.

I encourage you to get help even if you have to pay for it. The amount of time it can cut off your learning curve will be well worth the money spent, and the return on investment will be tenfold. It won't be inexpensive as most professionals are in the market and monitoring whatever positions they have and to mentor you means they need to take time away from what they need to be focused on so be prepared to pay if you want professional help.

The mentor I had and still call and ask questions to every now and then, trades a very large account and does very well. It is all he has ever done for a living all of his life. I did not have a mentor for live trading until I was already doing it and making some money consistently however as I said above if you can find someone who can help you from the start it will *greatly reduce* your learning curve.

As I said *you* are your own worst problem when you are just starting out in this business and a mentor can greatly help you from being a detriment to yourself and keep you from self-sabotaging your trading. To many times people come into this business with dollars signs rolling around in their eyes like some old cartoon.

As has been said before, this is not a get rich quick business unless you are a hedge fund, and using OPM (other people's money) and leverage or both. It is precisely the opposite for retail traders. It is a very slow growth of your equity curve and your business.

Don't get me wrong. You *can* and perhaps *may* make a lot of money in this business. Depending on the amount of capital you choose to deploy in the live market at any given time. The trader who mentored me is a full time trader who trades a *very large* account size. This business is all he has ever done for a living and the only "job" he has ever had. There are days where he pulls out five to ten thousand dollars or more. He is a former bond pit trader so he has firsthand knowledge of the inner workings of the market.

I actually never *had* a mentor until I was already trading live with real money. He would ask how I was doing and I would be cagy and answer "making a little" Interestingly, he does not trade anything like I do. He is more of a quant than anything else, he likes his numbers. I do *what* the smart money is doing *where* they are doing it from and make my money along with them *so should you*.

I am self-taught and self-made and did it all on my own which makes the success all the sweeter. All of the businesses I own I have started on my own with no help or money from anyone. *I just did it* and you can too.

This book affords readers who are brand new to swing trading and investing the opportunity to really learn and expand their knowledge base as new Forex traders from someone who came up on his own and trades and invests and trades with real money on a daily basis. This book should be a *must read* for novice and inexperienced traders looking to build on their foundations and strategies.

It is my hope that one day it could be taught as a course at all of the top business schools and should be *required reading* for anyone who has *zero* knowledge of trading and investing who wants to get into it and do it as a business. If you know someone who wants to trade please let them know about this book.

This book gives you a great idea of what it will really take to become a successful consistently profitable trader on a daily basis. There are zero shortcuts to success in this business and there is only fortune to be had by those who take the right approach and learn the business the right way from the first day. Anything else is not acceptable when your hard earned money is at stake *right*?

As far as all the rules and regulations of trading are concerned for individual self-directed traders I encourage you to know what ones are pertinent to the style of trading and investing you intend to do for your business. I cover a couple of them in this book however you must do your own due diligence on what is the best way to trade and invest for *you* once you have the information you need.

I hope you have enjoyed this bonus section as it will serve you well if you follow the advice I give in here. No one wants to spend a lot of time doing all the education and training to do this business only to find that they lose money right away. Making a comfortable living from investing and trading the financial markets is *completely possible* if prepared for in the right manner.

If you start off small a build on success you will have a much better chance of having long term success and longevity in the business.

Oh and one last thing.

Don't stay long too long!

Extra links

http://www.informedtrades.com/index.php has a huge amount of free courses for the brand new investor and trader.

This is a great *free* supply and demand learning thread http://www.forexfactory.com/showthread.php?t=4282 04

Here is a link to a video that teaches how to draw the proper type of lines around a supply and demand value area. https://www.youtube.com/watch?v=jRjdR_kPMyw

Much more information on Forex Futures can be found on the CME website, The CME is: www.cmegroup.com.

You can look at some historical charts and get data at http://www.macrotrends.net/

Here is a great link with a lot of frequently asked questions by brand new traders and investors. http://education.howthemarketworks.com/stocks/begi nner/practice-stock-trading-questions/ I encourage you to have a look and try to absorb a little bit of the basic information at a time. You don't need to know it all by heart verbatim however it can help you to understand some of the mechanics of how the markets work.

This link helps you to have a better understanding of how stocks are affected by supply and demand. http://www.investopedia.com/university/stocks/stocks 4.asp

The next links will really peel your eyes open and make you think if you really want to get into this business or not. All links provided in this section are working as of the writing of this book.

https://en.wikipedia.org/wiki/Fractional-reserve_banking

https://www.youtube.com/watch?v=TcGldf0UFXU this video is long and I suggest you watch it in 30 minute segments and then try to digest the data. It's scary because some of things the presenter is talking about happened in 2008 and he is talking about them in what I would guess by the clothing and cars is the 1980's. 2008 financial crisis had not even happened yet.

This next video will only compliment the one just above and you should watch it and pay strict attention to some of the things the people being interviewed are saying.

https://www.youtube.com/watch?v=z7nTplUffXg

I encourage you to share these last two videos with everyone you know and love.

Glossary
Glossary of terms and abbreviations

ATM = automated trade management

AMM = Automated Market Makers

AI/AO - All in all out

Base or basing = an area where price is moving sideways and price is in balance.

BP = Big or bigger picture

BO = break out

DD = Due diligence

EOD = End of day

EOT = End of trend

ERC = Expanded range candle

FUBAR = fleeced up beyond account recovery

HH = Higher High

HL = lower high

LL = lower low

LH = lower high

HFT = High frequency traders

IMO = in my opinion

IPO = Initial Public Offering

S&D = Supply and demand

SM = Smart money - banks, large institutions, hedge funds etc.

TMI = to much information

MTF = multiple time frame analysis

PT = profit target

SL = stop loss

FOMO = fear of missing out

TC = Trend confirmation

ONL = overnight low

ONH = overnight high

OB = over bought

OS = over sold

PA = Price action

PM = Profit margin

PDL = previous day's low

PDH = previous day's high

SPEC = speculator

S&R = support and resistance

Range bound = sideways price action

TF = time frame

Trending = PA is in an up or down trend

ROI = Return on investment

RTH = Regular trading hours

TA = Technical analysis

TL = trend line(s)

TOS = Think or Swim

VAP = value area proximity

<<<>>><<<>>>

Disclaimer

This book is for educational purposes only. Futures, options, equities, and spot currency trading have large potential risk and traders should be well-educated before putting real money at risk. You *must* be aware of the risks and willing to accept them in order to invest in all markets. *Never trade with money you can't afford to lose.* This book is neither a recommendation or solicitation, nor an offer to buy/sell a futures contract or currency.

Forex, futures, stock, and options trading *are not* appropriate for everyone. There is a substantial risk of loss associated with trading these markets. Losses *can* and *will* occur. *No* system or methodology *has ever* been developed that can guarantee profits or ensure freedom from losses. *No* representation or implication is being made that using the trading concepts methodology or system or the information in this book will generate profits or ensure freedom from losses.

HYPOTHETICAL OR SIMULATED PERFORMANCE RESULTS HAVE CERTAIN LIMITATIONS. UNLIKE AN ACTUAL PERFORMANCE RECORD, **SIMULATED RESULTS DO NOT REPRESENT ACTUAL TRADING**. ALSO, SINCE THE TRADES HAVE NOT BEEN EXECUTED, THE RESULTS MAY HAVE UNDER-OR-OVER COMPENSATED FOR THE IMPACT, IF ANY, OF CERTAIN MARKET FACTORS, SUCH AS LACK OF LIQUIDITY. SIMULATED TRADING PROGRAMS IN GENERAL ARE ALSO SUBJECT TO THE

FACT THAT THEY ARE DESIGNED WITH THE BENEFIT OF HINDSIGHT. NO REPRESENTATION IS BEING MADE THAT ANY ACCOUNT WILL OR IS LIKELY TO ACHIEVE PROFIT OR LOSSES SIMILAR TO THOSE SHOWN.

Made in the USA
Middletown, DE
15 October 2023